MAR 17 2011

How to Reconcile
Cultural Differences in Mergers,
Acquisitions, and Strategic Partnerships

THE
GLOBAL
M&A
TANGO

FONS TROMPENAARS
MAARTEN NIJHOFF ASSER

New York Chicago San Francisco Lisbon London Madrid Mexico City
Milan New Delhi San Juan Seoul Singapore Sydney Toronto

1 2 3 4 5 6 7 8 9 10 11 12 13 14 15   QFR/QFR   1 9 8 7 6 5 4 3 2 1 0

ISBN   978-0-07-176115-4
MHID   0-07-176115-2

This publication is designed to provide accurate and authoritative information in regard to the subject matter covered. It is sold with the understanding that neither the author nor the publisher is engaged in rendering legal, accounting, securities trading, or other professional services. If legal advice or other expert assistance is required, the services of a competent professional person should be sought.

> —*From a Declaration of Principles Jointly Adopted by a Committee of the American Bar Association and a Committee of Publishers and Associations*

McGraw-Hill books are available at special quantity discounts to use as premiums and sales promotions or for use in corporate training programs. To contact a representative, please e-mail us at bulksales@mcgraw-hill.com.

This book is printed on acid-free paper.

*To our parents, who taught us to dance
the tango of life*

CONTENTS

Foreword   vii
Acknowledgments   xi
The structure of this book   xiii

**PART I The context: Organizational integration,
          the human touch**   1

**PART II Introduction: The ten steps of
           the three phase framework**   21

Phase A: Creating the compelling business case   25

  Step 1: Re(de)fine vision and mission   25
  Step 2: Business challenges assessment through
  capturing business dilemmas   35
  Step 3: Purpose and values assessment   51
  Step 4: Choose values and behavior   76
  Step 5: The business case for integration   110

Phase B: Developing implementation strategy
through objectives and KPIs   113

  Step 6: Survey of key drivers   113
  Step 7: Develop implementation through
  objectives and key peformance indicators (KPIs)   117

Phase C: Realizing and rooting the benefits 135

Step 8: Systemic alignment 135
Step 9: Value and cultural awareness programs 150
Step 10: Continuous re-evaluation: monitoring
change towards the hyper-culture 151

PART III The business of relationships and dilemmas 153

Conclusion 185
Index 189

FOREWORD

Realizing the business benefits and creating wealth in an integration process is not easy because it demands the joining of values that are not easily joined. After all, if it was easy, it would often have been achieved in the past and yet it is well known that the majority of mergers and acquisitions fail to realize the expected benefits that were the original motive for doing them in the first place.

Plenty has been written about the challenges of pulling off a successful merger or acquisition, and the key issues are well known. What organizations need, though, is a practical framework for identifying the real issues and then resolving them in a structured and disciplined manner that satisfies all stakeholders. This is not simply to overcome differences in the legacy organizations but to positively revel in these differences and to harness them to even greater performance by integrating the best of both.

During the last twenty years it has become increasingly recognized that both national and organizational cultures need to be considered in modern business management. And, furthermore, leaders—even in local companies—will find they are leading and managing multicultural workforces. Many of the existing cultural conceptual frameworks essentially describe how different cultures give different meanings to relationships with other people, to their interaction with the environment, to time and to other similar cultural dimensions. We have learned to recognize and respect cultural differences. However, if we stop at these initial stages when trying to combine organizations, we run the risk of reinforcing cultural stereotypes. At present there is a lack of consistent, reliable and generalizable processes to create sustainable and integrated value from separate cultures.

This book presents leaders and managers with such a process. It is based on the proposition that cultures require commonality of vision, mission, strategy and values to create the trust which can deliver economic value from the relationships. There are non-stop culture clashes, and by culture the authors mean not simply the cultures of different nations, but those of different disciplines, functions, genders, classes, etc. Eliciting and analyzing the challenges that integrating parties generally face has become their particular area of interest and they describe a number of practical, research-based tools to assist in the endeavour of building human synergies.

While any integration program should include fundamental operational matters, we need to attend much more to managing the elements the new partners already share and to what divides them culturally. We also need to consider the leadership behaviors that are required to drive change and integration.

Modern global businesses require a lot of "effort" and understanding before they develop trust in one another's words and bonds. Many stakeholders are involved, from shareholders to employees, clients to management. Intercultural alliances involve differences in corporate cultures as well as national cultures and even differences in the cultures of competing functional disciplines like R&D versus marketing. More or less overt cultural differences can cause problems, but so can *perceptions* about each other's corporate and national cultures. The authors show how trust is developed across value dimensions and cultures by using the dilemma framework that they have honed over many years in their consulting practice and research.

Ultimate success, then, depends on our ability to enable people with different cultural perspectives to engage in meaningful and valuable discussions about the new business. The new approach offered in this book focuses on the value of the integration that stems from fusing two seemingly opposing value orientations into one, and benefiting exponentially from this fusion. The process starts and ends with our ability to recognize and respect differences from the outset. This approach internalizes and reconciles these differences to realize benefits that go well beyond the traditional merged value. Consequently it harnesses the organic growth potential and the innovative capability of the newly joined-up entity from the outset.

This book will help managers to understand and secure the best from their people. The Tango concept originally evolved to help people realize their potential through dance, but also to recognize the way they connect to their partner in a unified physical and mental couplet for the benefit of their relationship through their physical intimate movements and the hidden meanings of their long-term rapport. As they say, "it takes two to tango," and mergers and acquisitions need to be in the business of marriage and not simply weddings.

Professor Peter Woolliams, PhD
Senior Partner in Trompenaars Hampden-Turner Consulting
and Emeritus Professor, Anglia Ruskin University, UK

ACKNOWLEDGMENTS

Like any successful integration, the creation of this book was a true work of joining different client experiences, different consulting styles and approaches, and the invariable incongruous work schedules of the two authors, on top of incompatible time zones. While researching and writing this book, we sought to create value by combining value orientations that are not easily joined, most of the time writing during non face-to-face client work, but on airliners, trains, and buses or during car rides. We wrote about our ideas and experiences with clients when we could, while pursuing our lives with friends and loved ones, in the ultimate effort to connect and share the value of our experiences in the production of this book.

Yet, as is so often the case in resolving and integrating tough dilemmas, we could not have done this alone. Aside from the motivation we took from each other and so many of our client-friends as well as the inspiration that we obtained from the successful integrations that we supported, we could not have done this without the indomitable spirit and the endless support of our business partner Professor Peter Woolliams. Peter proved once again that it requires an objective, experienced professional to raise the level of integration of the author's contribution to this book. Peter worked quickly and diligently to get the best of both worldviews out of us. Without his ability to reconcile, this book would have not been as complete as it is. We are immensely proud of our accomplishment yet humble in the knowledge that we could not have done it without Peter's help.

We are continuously inspired by Charles Hampden-Turner, who developed and instructed us on dilemmas and dilemma theory as a value creating process for organizations, teams, and leaders. Charles continues to be the intellectual force behind many of our ideas and processes. This book would not have happened without his mentorship and inspiration.

There are a great number of other people that inspired us on the road to writing this book, first and foremost the leaders that opened up to reveal the dilemmas they and their executive teams faced. It is a sign of great leadership integrity to elicit and frame the dilemmas that one is facing at the top of the decision-making pyramid of any organization. We thank you all in spiral dynamics. Then there are the numerous friends and colleagues who root and contextualize our understanding and assist us on our path to greater simplicity of process and clarity of goals. We mention specifically Yury Boshyk, Bill Smillie, Anne Wargo, David Hurst, Sudhanshu Palsule, Monica Hill, Liz Melon, Tony Brown, Igor Tkachenko, Gert Jan Mulder, Paul Govers, Esha and Maya, and finally our Argentinian friends Julio Aranovitch and Patricia Janssen.

Fons Trompenaars and Maarten Nijhoff Asser

THE STRUCTURE
OF THIS BOOK

In Part I we focus on why there will always be business interest in engaging in mergers and acquisitions, what we define as organizational integration, and some of the main reasons for past failures.

In Part II we detail our approach to integrations, mergers, acquisitions, etc., and share our experience. Our approach is practical, concise and comprehensive and is backed up with case histories detailing our clients' experiences. The process flows from establishing the vision and values in line with the business case and follows a path to overcoming many of the common hindrances and obstacles to integration, particularly focusing on key drivers, objectives and KPIs, monitoring, evaluating and continuing to grow the NEWCO culture. We focus on the human relationships, the underlying values and behaviors of the leaders, AND how they support the strategic process. The leaders are the carriers of integrative change. As managers and teachers they transfer the knowledge from the two old entities into the new merged entity and establish the framework for growth.

We work within a dilemma framework, supporting the alignment of vision and values. We have developed a systemic and structured process that overcomes most of the common obstacles to successful integration and inspires organizations to develop through both innovative integration and organic growth.

In Part III we look more deeply into the business of relationship management and the associated dilemmas. We explore the issue of trust as a fundamental pillar of human integration and we touch on the basic assumptions and dimensions of human relationships and nature that form the analytical building blocks for the process of building trust and creating value in mergers.

Mergers provide a fertile breeding ground for dilemmas, and there must be a process for recognizing, respecting and reconciling them.

Reconciling the differences between the previously separate corporations builds a common platform for developing human capital, core values, talent management, leadership behavior, executive development and many ongoing business processes. Reconciliation of the toughest merger dilemmas enables the realization of the highest business value in both the short and long term.

PART I

The context: Organizational integration, the human touch

Global business expansion and development through mergers, acquisitions and strategic alliances is big business. Even in the wake of the financial crisis of 2008/2009, in a climate of banking difficulties and credit restrictions, more and more "share for share" deals are being proposed and effected.

Business is increasingly pursuing mergers, acquisitions and strategic alliances, not only to implement globalization strategies and necessary restructuring, but as a consequence of political, monetary and regulatory convergence. Global companies like P&G, J&J, IBM, GE, Pfizer and Cisco but also Tata & Sons, Mahindra & Mahindra, Haier, Lenovo, HSBC, and others all have an M&A strategy coupled with an organic growth strategy, enhancing growth and managing risk at the same time. Some will have partnerships with (former) competitors; others pursue integrations with other businesses in particular markets or product ventures. Some out- or in-source particular competencies to and from other organizations. Integrations in one form or another are a feature of the business world.

It's not easy . . .

Realizing the business benefits and creating wealth in an integration process is not a straightforward procedure. Integrations, in various forms, have been happening for decades, but with all that experience to draw on, two out of every three deals still don't achieve anywhere near the benefits that were initially anticipated. Although success rates of mergers and acquisitions are difficult to compare, as surveys in the area use a variety of assessment metrics, most point to a success rate of about one third, while some have found that only 20% of mergers and acquisitions are ultimately successful.[1]

Yet these low success rates do not appear to have curbed business enthusiasm for growing by refocusing through some type of integration. Given the current economic and financial climate, business leaders worldwide need to manage their resources and assets more tightly than before to build sustainable growth capabilities that can withstand downturns and emerge stronger than before.

Looking ahead, many pundits are predicting two conflicting trends, which have their origins in 2009. On the one hand we can observe a plethora of divestments and de-integration processes going on, in particular in the financial services industry. On the other we can see a round of increasing integrations and reorganizations under the pressure of global sustainability while global competitiveness increases. Bigger companies will abound but their strength will lie in their nimbleness and agility, not simply their scale or scope. Companies are realizing that they have to operate within a business ecology where interdependence, not independence or singular dependence, is the name of the game. Emerging markets will find more flexible capital sources, and conglomerates will leverage and alter their strategic approach to markets, forcing others to make rapid adjustments. Even the big US-based companies employ more and more people outside of the US and many generate more than half their income overseas (GE, Corning, IBM J&J, etc.). Indian, Chinese, and South African corporations are acquiring and integrating companies in the UK, the US, and across various parts of Asia and Africa (Old Mutual, Lenovo, Haier, Tata, Mahindra, etc.). Constant change, economic waves, financial bubbles, ambiguity, and risk measures will put a greater emphasis on the ability to

---

1 Booz Allen Hamilton study 2001, "Merger Integration: Delivering on the Promise"; and KPMG Consulting M&A Study Report 1999.

increase capacity, influence employees, collaborate with other entities across borders and boundaries, and integrate with former challengers.

Leaders will be faced with frequently recurring dilemmas or seeming trade-offs and will have to co-create solutions with their management teams and navigate their organizations in and out of complex strategic relationships with the ultimate goal of creating sustainable growth and value.

Definitions

Although they throw up similar dilemmas, mergers, acquisitions, and strategic partnerships are different types of union. An acquisition is when one company buys another and integrates it into its own organization. Mergers entail two organizations integrating into a third entity, even when the two original companies are of unequal size. There are many varieties of these integration formats, and many that "market" an outright acquisition as a merger in the public and/or private media. A strategic partnership or alliance may differ in this regard as there may only be an integration of a department or a smaller part of an organization for a particular purpose or defined project. We have also seen strategic partnerships that eventually end in a merger or acquisition.

For the purpose of this book, we will not differentiate between these different types of integration but will focus broadly on the cultural challenges underlying any kind of integration between organizations with a common purpose or goal, whatever that goal might be. With that in mind, when we refer here to a merger, we include acquisitions, partnerships, joint project teams, and any other instances where people (re)organize themselves to forge relationships between human or organizational competencies with the ultimate goal of getting more out of these relationships than the sum of their parts. We approach the challenges of integration from the principle of creating value out of human relationships and their alignment with strategic intent.

Merger optimism and the key elements of success and failure

KPMG (1999) and Booz Allen Hamilton (2001) have reported that more than two-thirds of mergers failed to live up to their own targets. However, in our consulting work we have seen some improvement in merger results in the past five years. The cynic might say that the main reason for this is that due to financial constraints purchase prices have become more realistic. There are some reports indicating that between 2005 and 2008 the average price for the acquired company was 16 times EBITDA (earnings before interest, taxes, depreciation and amortization).

There is also evidence that companies have become somewhat better at merging and have realized the need to place more focus on the human factor, relationship management, communication, trust, and a clear people process and human integration strategy. As a result of this new focus we have seen significant successes at IBM, Cisco, Compass (Catering), Johnson & Johnson, Linde AG and Vodafone. The Bank of America/Merrill Lynch merger will be an interesting case to watch, and we will see how well that merger process is going in the coming year.

At the same time as seeing signs of growing success, we have learned from our own research and clientele that there are many challenges ahead for merging organizations. Organizations will have problems if they fail to identify and focus on the key issues or to question (cultural) assumptions (both of these issues are discussed in detail below), or fail to assess and allocate appropriate resources.

Focus on the key issues

Traditionally, when we review the key issues in a merger, we distinguish between hard and soft issues. Managing these issues can in itself determine the success or failure of a merger. We look first at the hard issues.

Evaluating synergy and savings

Evaluating the synergies and savings for any merger or acquisition will confirm the direction the involved parties need to take and determine the steps and processes to be used. This is crucial in providing the necessary reassurance during the negotiations and early evaluation of the deal that the identified benefits are robust and can indeed be realized.

The synergy and savings evaluations process generally focuses on the areas of procurement, R&D investments, and new product development, as well as distribution channel and supply chain analysis. Examination of the operational cost reductions normally considers the area of headcount reduction, which is often the most difficult synergy to achieve and implement. Loss of staff is an inevitable outcome following the execution of a merger. What we learned from the KPMG (1999) study was that few companies move beyond statements of intent with regards to headcount reduction. On average 50% of managers will leave following the first year of any acquisition or merger, so it is vital to analyze precisely how and indeed whether the vision, mission and values of the NEWCO are completely aligned within the merger strategy. This important (re)alignment of business and cultural dilemmas forms the basis of our integration process. It is also extremely important to assess the inherent dilemmas underlying headcount reduction.

Project planning integration

The second most critical function is the integration of the project planning process as it provides the expression of the way in which the synergies from the combined organizations will be attained and gives tangible evidence that things are stable yet changing. The strategy of the merger is communicated through the selection of the project planning team and the goal setting. This process is carefully monitored by the general employee population in the organization—while not directly linked to the integration process itself, they are subject to it.

Due diligence

Due diligence is of fundamental importance to the non-operational pre-deal activities. It enables the acquirers to focus their attention upon market reviews, risk assessments, management competencies, and synergies to support the operational impact. It generally doesn't involve a full review of the (corporate) cultures of the two companies, but traditionally stays solely within the realm of financial measurement and reporting tools.

Questioning (cultural) assumptions

These challenges, traditionally referred to as the "soft issues," form the core around which we have created our human integration process.

Selecting the management team

Management teams for the NEWCO require exceptionally strong and visible leadership and direction to drive complex value realization. Generally, though, the selections are either made in great haste (e.g., Bank of America and Merrill Lynch) and demonstrate obvious power and title related choices, or too slowly with a severe loss of motivation and morale which often results in the loss of important management talent, not to mention market value as investors grow impatient over time. In this context, we need a stronger focus on the specific skills of the leaders initiating the merger and those who make up the integration management teams. These individuals need to be true reconcilers of differences and dilemmas of strategy, organizational structure and team culture. We have developed a framework for assessing and training such individuals in identifying tensions and dilemmas and providing reconciliation techniques which lead to integrated value at all levels.

Resolving cultural issues

In most studies the main reason given for merger failure is "cultural differences." These issues must be better addressed so that future mergers will succeed where others have failed. A systematic and triangulated approach to assessing cultural differences needs to be in place and communicated through the management ranks and beyond. There are many tools available to help in this, and we'll share a few of these later in the book, but importantly, we have found that it is not just about measuring cultural differences and/or resolving potential challenges.

Our consulting process always begins with identifying and prioritizing the key integration issues through multiple assessments. The problem with organizational and national cultural issues in general is that the underlying basic assumptions remain largely implicit and unspoken. We have spent 20 years refining ways of making these cultural issues explicit and prioritizing them. Using a consistent and well-researched method to elicit cultural issues, challenges and dilemmas in a merger early on can provide a major improvement over current integration processes. It is vital that the new culture that is being created takes the best of all worlds and supports the new strategic challenges.

Communication

Communication needs to be treated like any proper business process. It needs to be consistent, reliable, and repeatable. Leaders of industry know that any successful message will need to be reiterated many times in many different ways. Management teams cannot communicate too much. As the 1999 KPMG report concluded: "Communications to employees will have a greater detrimental effect on the deal's success than that to shareholders, suppliers or customers . . ."

Secondary level managers and lower level staff are often kept in the dark about the opportunities of the merger at their level, and are barely included in regular communications. It is immensely important to identify formal and informal ways of "working" the communications channels throughout the merger process. The organizations that prioritize communication plans as a central part of their overall integration process are much more likely to be successful in attaining merger success than those that see communication as just one of the many tasks to be undertaken in the merger process.

In most surveys, poor selection of the management team and failure to resolve cultural issues generally score very high among the reasons for merger failure, but evidence from our consultation work reveals that the communication problems often act as a multiplier on the other factors in determining success or failure. The ability to communicate effectively during a merger becomes increasingly important as merging organizations face dilemmas. Leaders need to create dilemma maps that identify and analyze the toughest merger challenges and communicate a strategic path for reconciling them. These maps integrate the need to build strategic alignment and commitment, while communicating a common language and supporting the vision. Dilemma maps become discussion models that lead to greater understanding amongst core project teams and other employees. We will elaborate on the power of these dilemma maps in detail later in the book.

Integration of process

We have found, in our own work on merger success, that each of these elements has a primary role to play in supporting success and enabling goals to be achieved. However, these key elements cannot maximize the potential benefits in isolation—**the activities must be brought together in a single integration process** that enables the NEWCO to maximize its post merger success.

A successful merger requires the same processes that any individual company requires:

- A vision and mission that indicate what the aims of the merger are;
- A purpose that indicates what the merged companies stand for;
- A strategy that identifies how the goals will be achieved;
- Strong values that direct the all-important relationships within and outside the company.

The many dilemmas and challenges that individualize the merger process make each merger unique. We need to acknowledge these unique cultures and dilemmas while providing a consistent, reliable and repeatable process to drive merger success.

Merger goals

We can't talk about merger success or failure without addressing the *measurement* of success and failure. Most research organizations focus primarily on shareholder value as the ultimate goal and measure of success. But if we focus exclusively on the financial benefits of the merger within a relatively short time frame using precise financial indicators such as the stock price and shareholder dividends, we overlook the various levels of complexity that provide more sustainable shareholder value. We have interviewed thousands of international business leaders and extensively reviewed the management literature and have found that many organizations are simultaneously managing at least five parallel goals at all times in their business cycle (numbers 3–7 in the list below). These five goals are contextualized by the overarching goals of the organization's vision and values, and the strategic purpose that supports this (1 and 2 below).

1   Achieving the (joined) vision;
2   Reaching strategic goals after the merger;
3   Improving overall business processes;
4   Being regarded as a "best place to work" in our industry and beyond;
5   Increasing and maintaining customer satisfaction ratings throughout the merger and beyond;
6   Maintaining and increasing overall contributions to society and general social, political and economic recognition;
7   All of which will result in increasing shareholder value.

These parallel goals create dilemmas and value tensions for the NEWCO that we will examine in detail when we look at the "Ten Golden Dilemmas."

The human touch: integrated value

Organizations are often acquired on the basis of their inherent valuation (shareholder value) rather than with the intention of achieving full integration of all human capabilities. A wider range of other expected benefits might include synergistic values (e.g., cross-selling, supply chain consolidation and economies of scale) or more direct strategic values (becoming market leaders, penetrating a ready-made customer base, etc.). However, the pre- and post-deal management too often focuses on the rapid exploitation of new opportunities within a mechanistic or financial due diligence mindset, on the assumption that delivering benefits simply requires the alignment of technical, operational and financial organizational systems and market approaches.[2]

In contrast, the human relationships part of the merger is generally underestimated and few due diligence methods assess the value of power and trust or adequately map out the new and old stakeholder relationship management processes, either inside or outside the newly created company structure. We appreciate that this trend may change as talent management teams take on more global roles and have their strategic growth goals linked to expansion and integration targets.

The need for a systemic and methodological framework of people integration

The failure of a merger to deliver the anticipated benefits can be tied to two main problems: payment of an over-optimistic price and the absence of a systemic and structured methodological framework for integration. The framework

---

2   KPMG Consulting M&A Study Report 1999.

provides a means of delivering the core business value of human resources. How do we assess the power and value of human interactions in the business context?

Without a framework that answers this key question, senior managers have no rationale for allocating human resources, prioritizing actions, or achieving synergies, except as they match these against financial and capital resources. However, as we have already pointed out, on a strictly financial or capital basis most mergers and acquisitions actually lose money and destroy capital over time.

Measuring the financial value of the human resource is fraught with difficulty as humans are invariably more dynamic and versatile than financial or capital resources. Hence it has proven difficult to measure the return on investment in human capital, although many have tried. The measurement itself is also a problem. How do you measure elements that are largely non-linear, intangible, and difficult to put on any metric scale in the first place, and subsequently measure the increase or decrease of their output over time?

We have developed a dynamic measure on a dual axis grid of two opposing value orientations that describes the value (current and ideal) of human decision-making ability.

When a German mining giant merged with a US-based mining company, the control over decision making imposed by the German leadership stifled US flexibility and autonomy. The US-based leaders wanted to execute a quick deal with another US entity that would enable them to buy in much needed technology and thereafter sell the mine onto a third party in the US. Their efforts were thwarted, as they required approval from the slow and steady German decision makers, who required input from a number of stakeholders including the employee council.

The challenge can be summarized as follows: On the one hand, we need a fast decision-making process if we are to benefit from rare market opportunities. On the other hand, we need a secure and steady decision-making process to build consensus amongst the various stakeholders. The extremes of this dilemma are effectively pathological manifestations of the underlying value orientations and are unsustainable, as each entirely rejects the alternative. The compromise position on this grid is what actually happened in this case. The US entity bought the third party and sold it instantly to another buyer without further content benefit, but with a financial gain from the transaction. The framing of the challenge is shown in figure 1.1.

After this event, the parties got together to frame and resolve the tensions that were revealed in the process of the deal. As the parties explored the dilemma they realized that the synergy of their opposing value orientations could reap huge benefits for the company. Now this is an excellent way of assessing the synergistic value of human capital. When leaders are working from the same map, and have a

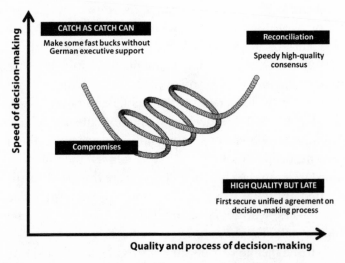

Figure 1.1 Legacy companies with different approaches to decision making

process for recognizing, respecting, and reconciling the challenges between them, integrated value can be attained and measured.

The above noteworthy example is based on two seemingly opposing value orientations. Such value orientations can be organized into differences/dualities, and as long as we put the dualities of value orientations together into "couples" where both sides are stated positively, we can measure the current status of the tensions between the two seemingly opposing values and "score" these on the dual axis grid.

Once we have established our starting point, we can also indicate an ideal point and potentially even indicate the path from current to ideal (as indicated above by the spiral). Using a dual axis grid allows us to measure the score differentials in blocks and place a value on the increase over time. We will elaborate on this approach later in the book.

The central thing to understand here is that values are differences and stem from tensions between two positive orientations towards, or interpretations of, a core value. Being able to dissect human activity and communication (decision making, negotiation, and presentation) and organize its intent and results on a map created on the basis of seemingly opposing value orientations is not just instructive, visionary and motivational but is also a serious attempt to identify and measure the value of human relationships and trust in merger and acquisitions and many other reorganizations and human relationships.

Mapping and measuring a human integration approach in the context of complex organizational changes has proven invaluable to the process of ultimate value creation, for which human interaction is responsible. The ability to integrate and multiply this effect across an organization in a consistent, reliable, and repeatable manner frequently leads to a competitive advantage for our clients.

Meta-dilemma of mergers and acquisitions

Throughout this book we will be using our two dimensional logic graphs to map integration challenges. We use an x-y grid where both extremes are shown, together with how they might be connected. We explain the justification and benefits of this approach in more detail later, but as an initial example, let's consider the meta-dilemma that summarizes two extreme paradigms of "acquiring" or "being acquired" in the example map shown in figure 1.2.

The "take over" axis is set against the "being overtaken" axis in a manner that instantly suggests that the two are not mutually exclusive and that an either/or approach will not optimize the situation. If we consider the "take over" axis and follow it to the end point on the grid, we end up in the space currently occupied by the "bear hug." Every extreme on this grid is described with an epithet or a characteristic that includes a positive sense (such as a hug) countered by its negative extreme (being squeezed). Mapped in this manner,

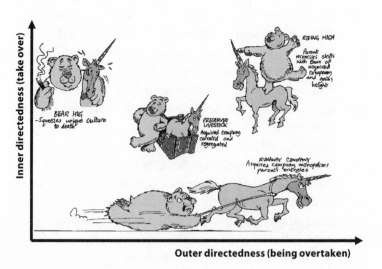

Figure 1.2 Strategy of managing cultural integration

we note that every extreme becomes pathological in and of itself. Although the "bear" culture acquired the "unicorn" culture for its uniqueness, applying its "bearish" ways will actually smother the special features of the acquired company. This behavior was common during the late 1990s and early in this century when, for example, GM and larger pharmaceuticals bought innovative companies. The GM way stamped out innovative, market-directed ideas within the acquired companies.

On the other side of the grid, we can see the "unicorn" culture running away with the bear behind it. Notice the anxious expression on the bear's face. Not exactly confident of its acquisition, is it? The middle ground (5,5) outlines a "compromise." Both parties have agreed to play it safe and split the difference. There are many ways to arrive at this stalemate position, which we frequently identify as "water with the wine," or "a little bit of both." There is no benefit from the integration and no learning transfers from the acquirer to the acquired or vice versa. Table 1.1 describes the different positions shown on the grid.

The extensive research evidence we have collected and triangulated with real world applications through our consulting, reveals that the 10,10 paradigm in the top right corner is where a sustainable future that delivers the business benefits of the intended merger or alliance can be realized. We call the pathway to this position the dilemma reconciliation process.

Of course, there are many ways to get there and many excellent examples. IBM and PWCC performed an integration dance of change based on former CEO Lou Gerstner's book *Who says elephants can't dance*, implying that Big Blue needed to be nimble enough to tango! For years Cisco followed a different path, by quietly sneaking into its acquired companies and taking out the "local" financial system and plugging in its own, leaving local management undisturbed

Table 1.1 Five categorical types of extreme behaviors in alliances or mergers

Paradigm	Grid reference	Epithet/Metaphor
First, we have the alliance in which one of the partners sticks to their own values and proclaims: "My values first!" and "I win, you lose!"	Position 1,10	Bear hug
The second type of response is to *abandon your own orientation and go native*. Here a "When in Rome, do as the Romans do" approach is adopted. Acting or keeping up such pretenses won't go unseen—you will be very much an amateur. Other cultures will mistrust you—and you won't be able to offer your own strengths to the merger marriage. Here the acquiring organization adopts the working practices and corporate culture of the organization they acquire.	Position 10,1	Runaway company
Third, we find the leadership in denial, avoiding and ignoring value dilemmas by operating at arm's length and assuming the synergy will take care of itself.	Position 1,1	Denial
Fourth, there is a type of new partnership where a compromise between values is found. Sometimes adopting the acquirer's way of doing things, and sometimes that of the organization being acquired. Synergies are not really achieved here.	Position 5,5	Preserved livestock
Finally, and for mergers/alliances/integrations that are more effective and realize and exceed the expected benefits, we find the reconciling alliance in which values are integrated to a higher level of integrity, where both sides improve beyond themselves and synergize into a new entity, with a much higher valuation than the sum of their former parts.	Position 10,10	Riding high

and focused on business development and sales. The global resource management power of Cisco drove the local innovative business, and integration opportunities could be assessed on a financially even keel.

Our validated questionnaires, structured interviews, and focus groups confirm that where parties can quickly reconcile and integrate their different perspectives, the expected benefits of the alliance or merger are achieved or even exceeded.

All cultures have their own integrity, which we do not want to lose. *We need others to be themselves if partnership and integration are to work.* This is why an approach that *reconciles differences* is required. Reconciliation enables us to be ourselves, yet to see and understand how alternative perspectives can enhance our own. It is more than just avoiding misunderstandings and blunders through poor communication. Reconciliation generates an integrated value because both parties contribute their strengths to the NEWCO.

Part II

Introduction:
The ten steps of the
three phase framework

Our central focus is enabling people with different cultural perspectives to engage in meaningful discussion. Our methodology uses dilemma thinking to bring people together to discover what they share and where they differ.

The meta-level

Our research and professional practice reveal that a genuine and successful integration process requires four components: recognition, respect, reconciliation (of both the business and cultural dilemmas resulting from these first two components), and, finally, realization—in which the business benefits of connecting different viewpoints are embedded throughout the organization.

When strategic, structural, systemic, human resource, supplier and client processes are aligned, maximum value will be obtained from the merger. Within this wider context, our approach can be defined as a process of reconciling divergent goals, values, and structural, functional, and cultural differences for maximum performance. As a result, the human (relationship) side will be fully integrated with the more technical aspects of the process.

Our process is supported by a number of validated instruments and tools that provide quantitative and qualitative diagnosis, monitoring of progress and hard evidence to inform decision making and resource allocations. As a result we work on assessed and elicited rather than assumed needs.

The full ten step process comprises three main phases; the steps are laid out in tables 2.1, dealing with phase A; 2.2, showing phase B; and 2.3, laying out phase C.

Table 2.1 A: Creating the (compelling) business case

Phase A activities	Goals	Means/tools
Step 1: Re(de)fine vision and mission	Truly integrate new organization	Revisit mission and values with "four whys?"
Step 2: Business challlenges assessment through business dilemas	Clarify new challenges through business dilemmas	Interviews validated by Webcue (elicit dilemmas)
Step 3: Purpose and values assessment	Define core values and key purpose for new integrated organization	Interviews validated by value surveys (PVP and OVP tools) Supporting workshop session to define key purpose
Step 4: Choose values and behavior	Link values with effective behaviors	Online diagnostic Webcues IAP and CCA tools + supporting interactive workshop(s)
Step 5: The business case for integration	Integrate business and values assessments for better business performance	Workshop sessions linking re-validated values with effective business case

Table 2.2 B: Developing implementation strategy, its objectives, and key performance indicators

Phase B activities	Goals	Means/tools
Step 6: Identification of key drivers	Design communications—customize the methodology and content of the cultural integration process, to provide executives with personal feedback	Analysis of the PVP and OVP assessment Coaching sessions Workshops on the DRP (dilemma reconciliation process) and developing KRIs (key reconciling indicators)
Step 7: Develop implementation strategy	Create clear objectives and indicators	"Causal" indicators that relate to values and behaviors "Output" indicators that relate directly to performance "Outcome" indicators that relate to the end results

Table 2.3 C: Developing systemic alignment and value awareness

Phase C activities	Goals	Means/tools
Step 8: Systemic alignment	Alignment of values with vision and mission	Individual and group cohesion workshops - Values to Behavior (V2B) - Structural alignment of systems and processes
Step 9: Value and culture awareness programs	Rooting awareness in the larger organization	Awareness/feedback against determined goals Personal development: e.g., blended learning through the ICP and CCOL
Step 10: Continuous re-evaluation	Monitoring (and controlling) change toward the hyper-culture	Individual and group deliverables - KRIs (achievement of key reconciling indicators) - OVP progress and personal development reports

PHASE A: CREATING THE COMPELLING BUSINESS CASE

The five steps of phase A are:

1 *Re(de)fine vision and mission*
2 *Business challenges assessment through capturing business dilemmas*
3 *Purpose and values assessment*
4 *Choose values and behavior*
5 *The business case for integration*

We will explore them in turn.

Step 1: Re(de)fine vision and mission

We have found that the first step in creating a successful integration is the creation of a compelling business case—integration is much simpler when there is a jointly defined vision. Thus, the purpose of this initial process phase is to derive and explicate a clear idea of the vision and mission for the newly created entity. At this point, the initial goals for the merger can be refined through extensive iterations which provide a check on whether the re(de)fined mission is still inspiring and motivating to the new leadership. It is also important that the shared values and behaviors of the organization support that vision.

This process has its origins in the work of Collins and Porras[1] who have clearly demonstrated that successful organizations need an alignment between their "envisioned future" and "core ideology," together comprising the organization's vision. Figure 2.1 summarizes their concept.

A well-conceived vision consists of two major components: *core ideology* and *envisioned future*. Core ideology, the *yin* in Collins and Porras's scheme, defines what an organization stands for and why it exists. In successful organizations *yin* is unchanging and complements *yang*, the envisioned future. The envisioned future is what we aspire to become, to achieve, to create.[2]

It is essential that the envisioned future is revisited with the new top leadership group and linked to the core motivation. A vision is determined, not given, and the process of defining it is often a great way to communicate and explore the strengths of both organizations and how they might be integrated in a way that is non-compromising. It also often reveals why an organization was purchased in the first place. And if the strategy is one of "riding high," the self-confidence of the acquired organization is also raised.

The main difference between the routes UniCredit and Linde AG took to integration (described below) is that Linde's CEO Reitzle invested time in frequent sessions with the old board of BOC to redesign the process. In this way the whole board was included. And in the end, that made all the difference.

After the main vision and mission of the NEWCO is (re)defined, there is a context for the leadership of the organization to be invited to assess its business and values. This is

---

1 Collins and Porras, *Built to Last*, 1994.
2 Collins and Porras, "Building your corporate vision," *HBR*, September–October 1996.

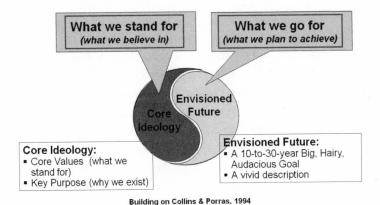

Building on Collins & Porras, 1994

Figure 2.1 Strategy of managing cultural integration

UniCredit

Allessandro Profumo, CEO of the large Italian bank UniCredit, is a visionary leader. His clarity of vision and mission has been instrumental in turning significant international acquisitions into successes.

UniCredit's vision is based on their determination to create a new way of banking by focusing on people as individuals, enhancing their potential and enabling them to achieve their goals. Their mission is to aim for excellence and consistently strive to be easy to deal with. As a "group," they adhere to commonly held principles and a distinct set of values based on integrity as a primary condition of sustainability, which makes it possible to transform profit into value for all stakeholders.

Employees are guided in their daily business by the "integrity charter," which sets out the core business principles. The charter was created as part of UniCredit's integration process, providing a very clear framework within which the many acquired banks in Central Europe, Germany's HVB and Aus-

tria's BACA could find their way. In the case of UniCredit, discussion around the creation of this vision and mission was restricted, but what was explored through extensive consultation were inputs that would make it possible to reconcile the major dilemmas that the integrated organizations had to face to make it a reality. This is further discussed below along with how it made UniCredit one of the largest European banks. Eventually the following Unicredit mission crystallized from this process:

We, UniCredit people, are committed to generating sustainable value for our customers. As a leading European bank, we are dedicated to the development of the communities in which we live, and to being a great place to work.

We aim for excellence and we consistently strive to be easy to deal with.

Linde AG

Dr. Reitzle, CEO of Linde AG, had a vision that his German-based conglomerate should become "the leading global gases and engineering group, admired for our people, who provide innovative solutions that make a difference to the world."

Linde AG was made up of a variety of related and unrelated businesses (including a material handling business segment, one of the world's largest manufacturers of forklifts and warehouse equipment). Decade after decade, Linde AG has touched and improved the lives of billions of people through the jobs, capability and wealth created by its core activities around the world, as well as through the products and services they supply to customers across a wide range of industries, from steel making to food production, waste-water treatment, environmental protection and health care.

However, because of the globalization of markets Dr. Reitzle was convinced that with the portfolio Linde AG had historically adopted, it was not possible to increase Linde's valuation by the capital markets and to realize his vision. First, the organization needed to concentrate on the gases and engineering business, deepening its knowledge and becoming less German-centric. After some major divestments they acquired the UK-based industrial gases company BOC Ltd. This organization was a logical candidate because it was very international and shareholder driven and so quite different from Linde AG. The only way for Linde AG to make a difference to the world through innovative solutions was to marry a candidate like BOC. The rest is history.

very often a top-down process, as was the original decision that prompted the merger or acquisition. We find that the most successful starting point for this discussion is the envisioned future and the BHAG (big, hairy, audacious goal).

The beauty of this early assessment of the business logic behind the integration is that management are working together from the outset to create a new, shared future. They begin with the question, "Why did we come together in the first place?" This works much better than the frequently observed behavior of looking at the differences first. Differences become more supportive of the integration process AFTER the shared boundaries are defined. Integrating diverse (business and value) orientations is not a matter of one party trying to understand and adapt to the ways of the other; it is a joint effort of mutual understanding and reconciliation.

The "big, hairy, audacious goal"

In this first step we begin by defining the "big, hairy, audacious goal" (BHAG). The BHAG is a bold mission statement to stimulate progress, such as "putting a man on the moon." According to the authors who first coined the phrase[3] the BHAG should:

- Be clear and compelling
- Act as a catalyst for team spirit
- Have a clear finish line
- Engage people
- Be tangible, energizing and highly focused
- Be easily understood by everyone

We are talking about inspiring and daring goals that can only be reached through extreme effort. Hamel and Prahalad[4] call them *stretched goals*.

Some good examples of BHAGs are:

- Become a $125 billion company by the year 2000 (Wal-Mart, 1990)
- Democratize the automobile (Ford Motor Company, early 1900s)
- Become the company known for changing the poor worldwide image of Japanese products (Sony, early 1950s)
- Become number one or number two in every market we serve and revolutionize this company to have the

---

3   Collins and Porras, "Building your corporate vision," *HBR*, September–October 1996.
4   Hamel, G. and Prahalad C. K., *Competing for the Future*, Harvard Business School Press, 2001.

strengths of a big company combined with the leanness and agility of a small company (General Electric Company, 1980s)

- Become the Nike of the cycling industry (Giro Sport Design, 1986)
- Powering the Human Network (Cisco Systems, 2009)
- Building a smarter planet (IBM, 2009)
- "Organize the world's information and make it universally accessible and useful" (Google)
- "A computer on every desk and in every home" (Microsoft)
- Become the "world's online marketplace" (eBay)

After the BHAG is defined, the integrating parties are encouraged to find the main areas where they can develop business synergies within their newly defined shared goal. In fact, they might (re)visit the main reason why the organizations united—perhaps their stretched goals were unattainable as separate entities.

The BHAG needs to be challenging, compelling and inclusive. It needs to bring all parties together as a team, impress them, and give them a shared feeling of pride: "We have the courage to formulate a bold shared goal and that is what brought us together in the first place." It shouldn't be either a dreamy blue-sky ambition or a basic strategic goal, because a stretching goal should be attainable only with as yet undefined and undiscovered forces.

It works well to use a cascading approach starting with the top management team (5–10 people) who work in small subgroups of 2–3 people preferably from across the organizations involved to jointly articulate their goals.

Approaches to the discovery and eliciting of the BHAG

There are several ways in which the management team can be stimulated to create a compelling BHAG. The use of questions is very effective:

- Which people have inspired you?
- What about the acquired company convinced you that it should be bought?
- What qualities do you most admire about the acquiring organization?
- What are the moments of truth in the organizations' histories that are most crucial to you?

Alternative approaches are described by Collins and Porras as "vivid descriptions," such as looking at the organization's history and discussing how it has rewritten the industry's essence. It can be effective to ask rhetorical questions like: "What might you see as the 'Most effective merger in 2015' on the front page of an Industry Magazine?" Or, "Describe what the organizations have done to combine their mutual strengths to make the most successful integration and why. Was it because of a combination of products and services, the implementation of a new joint business model and better processes, or the introduction of a new way of leading?"

Sometimes both organizations in an M&A already have defined stretched goals. It is a valuable exercise to ask the participants to combine both bold missions and see whether there are some possible synergies. To keep both or a variety of BHAGs is risky because the end scenario might be too diffuse. And it should never be treated like a "balanced scorecard" where different fields are given different KPIs. The exercise should end with one vivid description that inspires all team players.

People should be given a chance to participate in the creation of the BHAG and it should unite all involved.

A cascading process

Once the top team (5–10 people) has agreed on the BHAG, the time is ripe for validation through consultation with the next layers—often the extended board and then the top 100–150 managers. Through this process the BHAG gains quality and definition and, even more importantly, all parties involved participate in its creation.

It is important to invite top management to comment on the draft BHAG so that it becomes theirs, and for the statement to then be communicated throughout the organization and opened up for further comment. If the groups are large, an interactive discussion system like Chrystal can be

---

Case study showing best practice: Geodis

Geodis Wilson is part of the French Geodis Group, with SNCF—the French railroad company—as its main shareholder. With 26,000 employees in a network spanning 120 countries, the Geodis Group ranks among Europe's top five transport and logistics companies. Geodis Wilson is the result of the merger of Geodis Overseas, the air and sea freight arm of the Geodis Group; Dutch TNT Freight Management, formerly known as Wilson Logistics, a 164-year-old company with Scandinavian roots; and most recently Rohde & Liesenfeld. Geodis Wilson has inherited the best of several worlds: a global network, a drive for growth, the desire to develop services that work, and a "can-do" mentality when partnered with customers.

In 2007 the newly appointed CEO of Geodis Wilson invited us to give a presentation to the top 50 managers, representing at least 30 nationalities, about the typical characteristics of French culture and how it would affect the further internationalization of the organization. We refused the offer, because it would jeopardize the integration process by initiating all kinds of stereotypes. Instead we chose to present the differences amongst the variety of corporate cultures with our Organization Value Profiler (OVP) and Personal Value Profiler (PVP). The PVP looks at the personal values of the participants and it revealed much more congruence than the separate corporate cultural profiles of the organizations involved (from our OVP). This was the basis for the further support we offered some three months later in Amsterdam exclusively with the new board.

The board of Geodis Wilson consisted of six people, two Swedish, two Dutch, one French and one British. A one day program was designed to craft the first draft of a key purpose, core values and a BHAG. The board went out in three (different) pairs in three rounds representing different companies. After each round there was an animated discussion about the different viewpoints around the bold mission. The first draft BHAG was formulated as:

Geodis Wilson wants to be recognized as the best quality provider among peers, customers and employees.

In the same session the values and purpose were defined as supporting the accomplishment of the first draft BHAG.

This first draft was taken to the top 25 (extended board including country heads) who meet quarterly. They validated the first draft of the BHAG in preparation for the top 250 meeting. That meeting validated a similar BHAG:

> *Geodis Wilson is recognized as the best freight management service provider by customers, suppliers and employees.*
>
> *Using the group dialogue system we asked the top 250 to discuss what they liked about this BHAG and how it could be improved. This ensured that people from all the merged companies were involved.*
>
> *The process ended with a re-stated BHAG that was perceived to have been co-created by the top 250. The meeting ended with agreement on a roadmap of how the BHAG could be used as a source of inspiration for the development of the values and purpose of the Geodis Wilson freight division.*

very effective. People can give anonymous input at the same time as the BHAG is communicated downwards. The parties involved in the merger will feel their inputs were taken seriously in developing a bold new joint mission.

Step 2: Business challenges assessment through capturing business dilemmas

Defining the business dilemmas in the context of the (re)defined vision and mission is a very powerful process for assessing and supporting a business case in any strategic integration of organizations.

Why dilemmas? Well, because we find the key challenges owe their origin to the competing demands of different stakeholders and their different points of view and interests. Which do we choose? Hands-on or *laissez-faire*? Top down or bottom up? Centralization or decentralization? Do we go for quick wins from the merger or a real long-term sustainable future? Choosing one option at the expense of another or even a (lose-lose) compromise means we have to give up the benefits of one extreme viewpoint.

These dilemmas can be captured effectively through a combination of face-to-face interviews and on-line semi-structured questionnaires that we call "WebCue." Differences in strategic and operational business orientations can create problems when working in a multi-organization integration process. This is even more striking when we realize that people from different backgrounds, vocations, and organizational cultures have very different ways of working together and often forge different kinds of relationships.

The big picture

At this stage we can say that a genuine and successful integration process requires the four components and developmental phases that we mentioned earlier—namely:

1 Recognition of different business orientations;
2 Respect for those differences;
3 Reconciliation of business dilemmas resulting from the above two steps; and finally
4 Realization and rooting, in which the business benefits of connecting different orientations are embedded throughout the organization.

The following example illustrates how dilemmas can capture the core challenges of an integration process.

Attracted by its innovation capability, a large pharmaceutical firm buys a smaller company; the dilemma looks like this:

> *On the one hand we need to increase the size of our organization for distribution and economies of*

scale; whilst on the other hand we need to develop the innovative powers of "small is beautiful" and exploit flexibility.

If this is not seen as a dilemma, we have to ask why the larger organization didn't choose to grow organically.

Centralization versus decentralization is a common dilemma in integration scenarios. At Linde AG, a highly centralized German-based organization, one of the main arguments for buying BOC was its decentralized approach to international business in which leaders delegated their authority as deeply as possible into the organization. IBM, when acquiring PWC Consulting in 2003 experienced the same dilemma. If we look at the Campofrío Food Group, consisting of many locally operating brands, it is the same story.

The reconciliation of this key dilemma makes or breaks the success of the merger. Remember that a dilemma can be defined as two propositions that are in *apparent* tension. A dilemma describes a situation where there are two conflicting *good* and *desirable* options. When a global organization is faced with the dilemma of whether to centralize or to decentralize business activities, there are four possible choices:

1 Centralize—this is the "head office dictates" paradigm.
2 Decentralize—otherwise summed up as "going native."
3 Compromise—each side gives something up to achieve a common goal.
4 Reconcile—much more challenging! And at first sight impossible. The key question is what do we need to centralize in order to allow for more decentralized activities? When two apparently opposing views are reconciled so that instead of "either/or" or "and/and"

thinking, a "through/through" solution is achieved, new value is created by combining the best of both.

Our dilemma reconciliation framework is a unique method of solving such problems. It is a way of looking at a variety of choices that organizations have to make for both strategic and operational effectiveness. It is a way of clarifying the difficult choices organizations have to make to balance, or even better combine, the "local" and "global" orientations they face. As such it is an invitation to create synergies. To be able to take both centralized and decentralized strategies and integrate these at a higher level is the strength of dilemma reconciliation.

Business dilemmas that manifest in mergers

Many business dilemmas are inherent in the different ways of working, better known as the culture of the legacy organizations. It is a sign of healthy integration when dilemmas are approached well and processed in a manner that reflects the complementarities between the entities.

With Linde and BOC we observed these dilemmas:

- We need to supply (global or standardized) products/ services vs. We need to supply products/services that respond to local tastes and needs.
- We need to develop our people vs. We need to keep people focused on delivering results.

In these cases dilemma reconciliation was crucial to the success of the NEWCO.

When UniCredit was integrating the German HVB and the Austrian BACA organizations they found the following dilemma crucial:

- Becoming a "Truly European Bank" vs. Maintaining close local relationships with clients/customers as a multi-local bank.

From UniCredit's meta-strategic dilemma some related dilemmas could be formulated, such as:

- Centralized vs. Decentralized excellence.
- How to integrate different European cultural traits (Italian HQ vs. Other European cultural traits).
- Ante-chambering meetings vs. Equal opportunities to contribute.
- Independence vs. Accountability.
- Proclaimed values vs. Opportunistic behavior.
- Subtlety vs. Communicability.
- Entrepreneurial flair vs. Clear codification.

Similarly, when Geodis bought TNT Express in 2007 the following dilemmas arose:

- We need to achieve short-term financial objectives vs. We need to develop a mid/long-term strategy.
- We need to grow bigger for economies of scale and to match global customer requirements vs. We need to grow better so we don't slide behind the competition.
- We need to standardize our processes to raise productivity vs. We want to be flexible to better answer customer demands.
- We need a clear and focused IT strategy vs. We need to keep numerous disparate systems running in the short term.
- We must grow the business by acquisitions and increased efficiencies vs. We should keep employee motivation high during uncertain times.

Global Computer and Consulting Services Company merger

In our integration work with a large computer and information-technology company and a premier consulting company, we elicited over 175 dilemmas and clustered them into seven major dilemma groupings that could subsequently be addressed by integration teams. We also supported 25 executive workshops to support local integration challenges in 25 global locations, where teams competed to provide the best solution to the most important dilemmas. Major dilemmas were noted, such as:

- *We need to optimize utilization of people vs. We need to be more innovative in providing new solutions to meet our clients' needs.*
- *We need to sell solutions to clients now vs. We need to implement high quality services fast.*
- *Relationship driven organization vs. Transaction driven organization.*
- *Operation through line managers vs. Functional support by business advisers.*
- *Experience and subjective judgment vs. Process- and rule-based ways of working.*
- *Work—Life balance.*
- *Hiring and motivating the best and brightest vs. Maintaining the best current performers.*

We managed to categorize a great number of the dilemmas and linked these to the core values of the organization. In this way, the core values were enriched by the reconciliations of the dilemmas that inspired them. Dilemma thinking and reconciliation became a common language that was subsequently adopted in many of the acquirer's customer relationships. Framing the acquirer's offerings versus the customer's needs and subsequently co-creating the reconciliation became a major driver for innovative solutions and services. Furthermore, it became apparent that some dilemmas in the US had already been addressed and resolved in different, previously unconnected corporate units in South Korea!

Reconciliation of business dilemmas, or assessing integration potential

The process of reconciling business dilemmas touches the very core of the integration strategy. The highest chances of success are found where there is a conscious effort to harness the strength of each of the legacy organizations. We guide participants through a dilemma reconciliation process which is based on the following elements:

- Identifying the dilemma.
- Charting the dilemma to make it more concrete; labelling the axes reflecting the opposing positions (positive or neutral) and plotting the positions of the actors.
- Stretching the dilemma by describing the positives and negatives of each side.
- Making epithets to characterize the sweet or sour in each of the extreme boxes.
- Reconciling the dilemma by asking how value A can support value B and vice versa.
- Developing an action plan for recognizing potential obstacles and plan for monitoring.

Geodis Wilson case

In their integration process, Geodis Wilson was very clear about the need to combine the achievement of short-term financial objectives (which was a great strength of TNT-Express) and the need to develop a mid/long-term secure strategy—the forte of their French parent Geodis. This reconciliation would make the organization much more resilient. This dilemma was discussed at a meeting in Paris between the country heads and the management team.

The end result is shown in figure 2.2.

The beauty of the discussion framework was that the positives and negatives of both approaches were openly discussed without excessive value judgment. The reconciliation of "being more selective in their investment strategy" was highly appreciated by all participants.

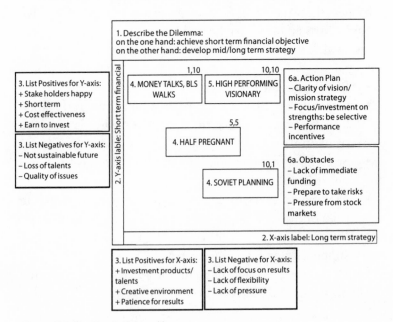

Figure 2.2 The Geodis Wilson dilemma

Selecting the investment decisions based on how they could harness short-term results whilst realizing the longer-term vision was an invitation to combine the best of both worlds and a great opportunity to avoid the stereotypes about the negatives of both legacy approaches.

Global Computer and Consulting Services Company merger

We facilitated many sessions for a large global consulting services company while they were trying to integrate the consulting branches under the umbrella of their "Role of the Leader" program.

A frequently occurring dilemma is the need for a sales oriented culture (as developed by the global computer services company) and at the same time a need for a service culture (traditionally a strong point of the large consulting services firm).

The various groups around the globe that considered this dilemma recognized it as being fundamental to their future working and it was reconciled in a variety of ways. Figure 2.3 shows one example.

Another important dilemma was in the area of people empowerment versus control by the company. It was crucial for the leadership that this was resolved.

Traditional computer company employees were accustomed to demonstrating loyalty to the parent organization and leadership. At the consulting services company, it was normal to challenge leadership. But in coming together, which model should be applied? This was very much a make or break dilemma for the NEWCO.

In the beginning there was a lot of disdain from each partner about the core values of the other. The stereo-

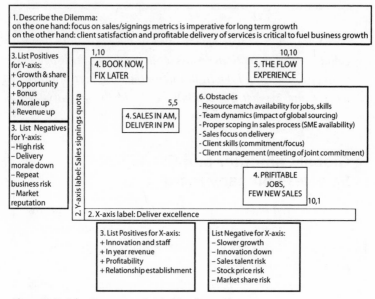

Figure 2.3 Sales Contracts vs. Service Excellence dilemma

typed long-term career hero on the one end of the spectrum was (as might be expected) very often pictured as a
staid, risk avoidant "bureaucrat" and the equally stere-
otyped well-connected consulting executive was seen
as an overpaid artist, shooting from the hip. These two
stereotypes were captured in the epithets "slow dictatorship," pictured as an elephant for the typical computer
company leader, and the "wild, wild West," represented
by dancers for the consulting services company partner.
Obviously there were a lot of worries that the elephant
would squash the dancers!

In the event, the DRP opened a dialogue in which
a wonderful metaphor was created: a group of dancers
protected by a net held by the elephants, as shown in figure 2.4.

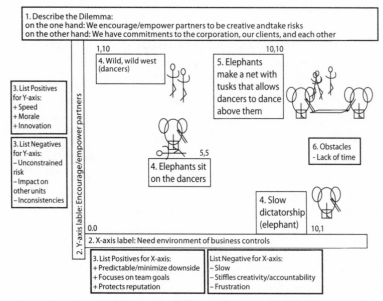

Figure 2.4 The reconciliation of the "wild, wild West" with the "Slow Dictatorship"

Beauty case

This case concerns a situation involving two anonymous organizations. Both are Dutch management consultancies. The "P Inc" organization has 15 consultants and 10 support staff. Though based in the Netherlands PI has many international clients. The founders and owners of the organization are thought leaders in the area of change management and leadership development, do research in the area, and publish books. Their work is known worldwide and marketing is predominantly done by picking up the phone.

During the last five years PI didn't grow more then 5–10% annually beyond broad expectations. Most disappointments at PI were caused by the fact that the clients loved the creative interventions, but further implementations were often hindered by non-scalability and lack of people to undertake the actual delivery and execution.

In short, PI is an inspiring organization with a challenge in execution. In 2007, after some years of searching, PI found a partner, "OL Ltd." This very successful Dutch consulting firm primarily operates in the Dutch market. Similar in size to PI its particular strength is staff engagement diagnostics and performance and helping organizations to implement change processes through web enabled chat. The ownership structure was quite different from PI since the shareholders (five in number) were separated from the management. In PI the two founders were main shareholders.

The management teams had a common vision for the NEWCO after integration. As a joint entity they would be able to serve the market from initial inspiring intervention at top management level through to execution at all levels that followed. The main differences between OL and PI were best captured by:

- *The push of cutting edge products and unique services vs. The pull of scalable and reliable ongoing services and diagnostics.*
- *The offering of globally significant services to an international clientele vs. The offering of a solid Dutch service to intimate clients.*
- *The nurturing of creative individuals vs. The development of ever better team work.*
- *The continuous development of people vs. The returns for shareholders.*

During the integration process all the consultants and support staff gathered and discussed the various versions of these business dilemmas in mixed groups. The results were very encouraging and helped to integrate the variety of perspectives and strengths of both organizations.

The first dilemma's reconciliation is shown in figure 2.5.

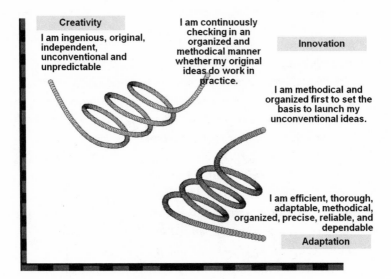

Figure 2.5 The reconciliation between creativity and adaptation

There was real excitement when the OL consultants explained the positives and negatives of their long-term relationships with their clients. Though the predictability and reliability was helping them to fine-tune the products to perfection, it was also seen as hindering the learning curve. The consultants of PI said they learned continuously but had great difficulty in standardizing what they had learned, leading to high development costs. The reconciliation was found in deciphering the essence that connected all the unique PI products. Because of the contrast that the more disciplined OL displayed, the PI consultants realized that the unique contributions of their founders gave them a methodology that was often ignored. OL consultants presented their highly centralized approach to their services and their focus on having all proposals scanned and edited by their CEO. "Eureka," said one of the PI consultants, "if *we structure all our proposals in a standardized way and have them assessed by our teams for similar methodologies that come up across all our work we will have a better chance of mass-customizing." The reconciliation of this dilemma is shown in figure 2.6.*

The reconciliation of this dilemma was crucial for the success of the merger. The challenging question was: "how could the PI consulting offering be extended and enriched by the standardized, mostly Dutch services and how could the OL consulting services take advantage of the international markets that were open but untapped?" On the first challenge, a lot of effort was put into the enrichment of the services by looking at how the Dutch services of OL, more focused on internet chats and benchmark diagnos-

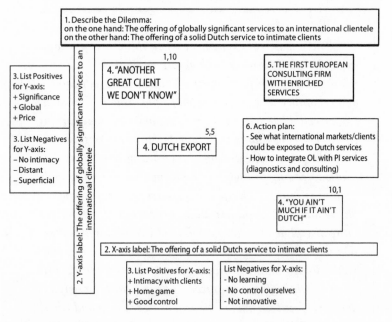

Figure 2.6 Global vs. local

tics, could upgrade the more touch-and-go offerings for the international organizations. In fact, the first experiments were highly appreciated by the international firms because they saw that the PI services could be better implemented and monitored because of the OL service extensions. On the second challenge a process approach was implemented. With every PI type of proposal an OL consultant was asked to see how their services could be added to or even better integrated into the more traditional proposal. The total turnover of the new PIOL organization went up by 23% in the first year and 41% in the second, now topping 20 million Euros annually.

Integrating opposites as a continuous and creative dialogue

Any integration process will throw up similar dilemmas in many areas—be it HR, loyalty programs, IT or finance. The process we facilitate generates a "creative space," where the ultimate solution is significantly better than any initial one-dimensional response. We call this the area where synergies are realized.

In this space a very intense and rewarding process of dialogue between the different organizational units—both operating companies and holdings—takes place. This synergistic process is of long-lasting value.

We have found that people succeed in achieving synergies, not because they are good at choosing one side over the other, but because they are able to reconcile seemingly opposing values. Integrating two desirable aims, which were in tension, creates a new, enriched reality. So in the case of the global computer services company that acquired a global consulting services company, the choice wasn't whether a sales or a service culture would make a better company. The challenge was, "How can we use a more sophisticated service culture so we can sell more?" and vice versa.

In the case of UniCredit, there was no need for a choice between being an Italian Bank with local characteristics and becoming a pan-European bank without anything Italian. Their approach focused on how the NEWCO could become a pan-European bank with an Italian footprint and how the best NEWCO offer in Italy could be a springboard for the other European activities.

And finally, in the case of the European consulting firm, we saw that mass customization and a transnational European approach made the organization unique by combining the best features of each of the units.

Organizations that are able to reconcile their differences will have created competitive advantage. If they do not, they will end up amongst the 70% of mergers that fail. But, most importantly, the DRP process invites the parties involved to participate in a creative dialogue rather than just complaining about each other in the corridor.

The specific steps in the reconciliation process need to be followed in a disciplined manner so that the process "equalizes" the game. Every party should contribute, regardless of whether they are the buyer or the bought, the smaller or the larger.

It is important to address both the business case for the integration and the cultural issues in this early stage. It is simpler to make the business case because it can be demonstrated in the financial results or key performance indicators such as ROI, employee retention, market share and customer satisfaction, etc. But the cultural case for vision, values, mission and key purpose is what really creates the motivation for the NEWCO to succeed.

Step 3: Purpose and values assessment

Having established the envisioned future and assessed the business case the road is clear to begin an organization-wide base assessment of personal, current and ideal cultural values. The measure of these values should be whether they will support the envisioned future for the NEWCO. This constitutes the third step in phase A.

Finding purpose

Here again it is effective to start with the larger context and ask the top group why they exist as a new entity. This is better known as the **PURPOSE** of the organization, its *raison d'être*:

- Why are we here?
- What can we offer our clients now that we are working together?

Initially this might need a little push beyond thinking in terms of "making more profit" or "having more products to offer." One needs to go to the ultimate desired state and not be afraid of exaggerating through brainstorming. Collins and Porras have called this the "key purpose" of an organization, and they characterize it with the following fundamental reasons for being:

- A guiding star on the horizon which we will ever pursue, but never reach . . .
- That which guides and inspires us . . .
- That which gives meaning to the work one is doing for an organization.

This is not to be confused with specific targets and business strategies, actual services or the markets one is now serving. To find the purpose of the new organization one must think beyond everyday occupations: if we have no aim beyond living our daily life as we already do, then there is no potential for growth and there is a risk of standstill. As Sensei Master Kenshiro Abbe 7th Dan reminds us:

立って静止画に後れを取ると同じです

"standing still is the same as lagging behind."

It is also important to avoid elevating profit making so that it becomes the highest aim of a company. Certainly, without money an organization cannot exist. But does that mean that money is the ultimate reason for being?

Discovering the (key) purpose

How does one discover the (key) purpose of an organization, its higher goal? Although no quick fix exists, we can try different approaches to discovering the ultimate nature of the organization. These can be applied separately or in combination. In the framework summarized below we have listed the different approach routes as consecutive steps.

It is fruitful to begin with discovering the specific identity characteristics of the organization. Begin by referring back to the findings from the original assessment of (combined) business opportunities. Review what is specific to the organization. Try to be as concrete as possible. Does the organization have particular products or services, qualities or skills? Try to define entrenched behavior and communication patterns, and think about their applicability to the newly created organization.

Then it is time to ask what the ambitions for the new organization are, what motivates the colleagues, and what makes a difference *vis à vis* the competitors and other stakeholders. Concern for realism should not hinder this exercise.

How to elicit the key purpose

We often begin with the so-called "five times why" exercise. This starts with a statement such as: "We provide quality products at the lowest possible prices." To which we might say: "*Why* is it so important to provide quality products at the lowest possible prices?" A more fundamental reason is given, and again is challenged: "*Why* is it so important to allow our clients to minimize the cost of their purchases?" Continued challenging of the weakness of any statement ultimately elicits what Peter Checkland calls the "root definition."[5]

Repeated questioning helps to elicit the very core of the fundamental purpose. "*Why*" is very important in making sure organizations follow their bold mission and envisioned future. "*Why* do we make furniture?" or, "*Why* do we want to consult big organizations?" The purpose anchors the ultimate meaning. The process is most successful when it combines the abstract and the concrete—the visionary and the practical.

Confront the group with questions relating to heritage: "What would be lost if the organization ceased to exist?" "Who would mourn our passing?" Such questions can generate responses that reveal the characteristics that distinguish one organization from all the others.

After these exercises have been completed, the (key) purpose of the organization can be articulated. This must

---

5   Checkland P., *Learning for Action*, John Wiley, 2006.

Campofrío Food Group

When Groupe Smithfield and Campofrío merged in early 2009, the Paris and Madrid based CEOs and chairman discussed and formulated a vision statement containing both mission and purpose elements. The first meeting with the Leadership Team and the management teams of the local IOCs discussed these first draft ideas.

The draft vision statement was:

"To be recognized by all stakeholders as one of Europe's leading food companies, offering a variety of high quality products which contribute to improving the quality of life and health of our consumers."

When the larger management team was asked for a response to this statement a variety of comments were made. Here are some of their responses to the question "why?"

- *"We need this in order to attain a position of admired company, a reference point within Europe (Top 10), in order to attract the best people."*
- *"We need to offer, through constant innovation, a variety of food products that contribute to improving the quality of life and health of our customers."*
- *"We capture the value of diversity (to enhance the quality of the product experience we offer)."*
- *"Because we want to inspire the industry, we are trend setters."*
- *"We like to behave like entrepreneurs and act fast; we are accountable for our results."*
- *"We respect the relationships with our customers, suppliers and colleagues."*

One of the marketing managers said: "Why not summarize our purpose as: "TASTY MOMENTS EVERY DAY, EVERYWHERE." This was popular because it was inspirational.

> *During the meeting, notes were taken and a next round of validation was done in different countries applying the same methodology. All the inputs were given serious consideration.*
>
> *The final version was:*
>
> *"To become one of Europe's most admired and successful leaders of quality food products by 2015, earning customers' preference and loyalty by providing them with delicious and nutritious choices for both everyday and special occasions that bring joy and health to the table."*

be formulated in a clear and concise way. The final statement should avoid the cryptic, cliché and trivialization. Remember, this is the very essence of the company. It must immediately inspire people.

The process of rolling out the purpose by engaging more members of the organization, across all legacy companies, creates bonding around what the NEWCO will share. As we saw in the case of Campofrío and Smithfields, the validating sessions contribute significantly to increasing commitment to the purpose. This is one of the reasons we advise companies to avoid choosing the existing purpose of one of the legacy organizations. If it is such a good purpose that it should be adopted for the NEWCO, then it will bubble to the surface anyway.

Culture and values

Once the (bold) mission and the (key) purpose have been formulated it is time to look at the values of the organization(s).

Both the purpose and mission are supported by the values. It is in purpose and mission that values and norms originate and certain types of behaviors are activated. "Values"

Beauty case: Part 2 . . .

And how did the PI/OL integration process, discussed above, proceed? The identification of the purpose was facilitated with OL's technology (called "internet-chat"). Everyone was invited to enter concepts, words or sentences that they saw as crucial to the existence of the NEWCO. There was only one criterion—they needed to support the vision of a research-driven, global and European consulting organization that translates values into performance. The following keywords were selected: connecting, perform-ance, consulting, viewpoints, reconciliation, diagnostics and sustainable.

Using these words, a key purpose was formulated:

To help organizations to recognize and connect dif-ferent (cultural) viewpoints leading to higher sustainable performance.

From this moment, people felt unity between the two groups. One commented: "Yes, I know there are differ-ences, but we need them if this organization is to attain its purpose. The energy it gives is amazing."

---

are the good and bad, "norms" the right and wrong. And behaviors are just expressions of that.

Corporate cultures develop their own values and behaviors. Values help support their functions, but more than that, they help organizations to survive in a harsh busi-ness climate and to achieve the goals they have set. Val-ues are functional and should be linked to the mission of the organization. When two or more organizations come together you can't ignore the deep structure their values represent. It would be naive to suggest that one set of values is superior to the other. All values have a reason for existence that cannot be ignored. In the process we describe below we take this as a starting point for the way forward.

Cultural diversity expresses itself in viewpoints and values, in operational priorities, and in ways of doing things. In our experience working with organizations facing complexity caused by cross-border M&A, we have found that issues rooted in cultural differences are best formulated as dilemmas because this approach allows the tensions that arise between different cultures to be explored.

Since culture is a key human driver of organizational performance, in any integration process, people from diverse backgrounds differ in the specific solutions they choose for universally shared business issues. Thus we find differences in management style, decision-making processes, communication styles, client orientation, reward mechanisms, etc.

Measurements: Our Organization Value Profiler (OVP)

Culture is to the organization what personality is to the individual—a hidden yet unifying theme providing meaning and direction that exerts a decisive influence on the overall ability of the organization to deal with the M&A challenges and dilemmas. Corporate culture has a profound effect on an organization's effectiveness, because it influences how decisions are made, how human resources are used, and how the organization responds to the environment.

We use our OVP (Organization Value Profiler) to identify the similarities and differences of the organizational cultures involved and the values of the existing organizations that will challenge and influence the merger or acquisition. The OVP enables participants to review and examine the interpretations employees give to relationships with each other and with the organization as a whole.

Unlike other corporate culture diagnostic tools, the OVP goes beyond simple diagnosis and serves as the basis for the reconciliation of the key tensions that arise in mergers/acquisitions, strategic change, diversity, globalization, etc. It is also designed to be "culture free"—that is, applicable to a diverse range of organizational cultures across the world. We have seen too many other models that display an Anglo-Saxon or US signature and have only been validated in the (national) cultures where they were developed.

The OVP is able to diagnose the different corporate cultures of the parties engaged in the integration process and will clearly show the value dilemmas that the new group is facing. It is an organizational culture scan that assesses the degree of formalization and flexibility, hierarchy and openness in the environment. It still has our underlying four quadrant model of corporate culture as shown in figure 2.7 and described below, but further sub-divides each quadrant leading to a full 12 segment model.

Incubator

Essence: A low degree of both centralization and formalization. In this culture, the individualization of all related individuals is one of the most important features. The organization exists only to serve the needs of its members. And its members are motivated by learning on the job and personal development.

Main characteristics:
- Person-oriented
- Power of the individual
- Management-by-passion

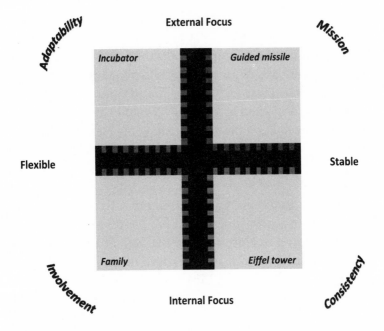

Figure 2.7 The four segments of the OVP model

- Commitment to oneself
- Professional recognition
- Self-realization

Main orientations:
- Things are done in ways that are very flexible and easy to change; work is done in flexible networks in which personal development is paramount.
- People have a deep understanding of customer/client wants and needs; customer/client input directly influences our decisions. Risk taking and innovation are encouraged and rewarded; people develop their potential by continuously learning.

Guided Missile

Essence: A low degree of centralization and a high degree of formalization. At its ideal, this rational culture is task and project oriented. "Getting the job done" with "the right person in the right place" are favorite expressions. Organizational relationships are very result-oriented, based on rational and instrumental considerations, and are limited to the specific functional aspects of the persons involved.

Achievement and effectiveness are weighed above the demands of authority, procedures or people. Authority and responsibility are placed where the qualifications lie, and they may shift rapidly as the nature of the task changes. Everything in the Guided Missile culture is subordinated to an all-encompassing goal.

Main characteristics:
- Task orientation
- Power of knowledge/expertise
- Management-by-objectives
- Commitment to tasks
- Effectiveness
- Pay-for-performance

Main orientations:
- Vision and values excites and motivates for employees; there is a focus on achieving goals and producing results.
- Work is organized so that each person can see the link between his or her work and the contribution to delivering tasks of the organization; feedback is given frequently on how well tasks and targets are met.
- Delivering short-term shareholder value is prime; initiative develops when people anticipate it will create shareholder value in the near future.

Family

Essence: A high degree of centralization and a low degree of formalization. It generally reflects a highly personalized organization and is predominantly power-oriented. Employees in the "family" seem to interact around the centralized power of the father or mother. The power of the organization is based on an autocratic leader who—like a spider in a web—directs the organization. There are few rules and thus little bureaucracy.

Main characteristics:
- Power orientation
- Power of network
- Personal relationships
- Management-by-subjectives
- Affinity/trust
- Promotion

Main orientations:
- Loyalty, commitment and trust between staff and the organization are considered important; information is shared widely so that everyone can get the information needed when required.
- There is a high concern for the relationship between people; knowing who is as important than knowing how.
- There is a high degree of team spirit even across different parts of the organization; one strives for involving people so consensus is reached.

Eiffel Tower

Essence: high degree of formalization, together with a high degree of centralization. This type of culture is steep, stately, and very robust. Control is exercised through systems of rules, legalistic procedures, responsibilities, and assigned rights. Bureaucracy makes this organization quite inflexible. Respect for authority is based on the respect for functional position and status. The bureau or desk has depersonalized authority. Expertise and related formal titles are very much appreciated.

Main characteristics:
- Role orientation
- Power of position/role
- Management-by-job-description/evaluation
- Rules and procedures
- Order and predictability
- Expertise

Main orientations:
- Staff is striving for structural efficiency; there is a focus on doing things in an economical way using know-how; people work in a stable and structured place with an atmosphere of efficiency.
- There is great concern for skills and professional development of people; the professional capability of people is constantly improving. Main loyalty is to the profession.
- The focus on the perfect structure means that each person has a clear division of functions and responsibilities in the organization; issues are settled by referring to rules, procedures and definitions of responsibility.

The four segments represent how the organization orientates itself to four basic processes in terms of task/strategy/mission, role/efficiency/consistency, power/human relations/involvement and person/learning/adaptability. Within each of the sub-segments we explore specific aspects that together determine the major orientations.

The design of the questionnaire reflects our underlying philosophy that bipolar scales (i.e., more of one meaning less than the other) are fundamentally inappropriate for the type of assessments we are making. We undertook extensive formal research and field testing to finalize the questions, including Cronbach Alpha reliability analysis and triangulation with face-to-face and online semi-structured interviews.

Because of the way the OVP works, it is possible to score highly on all four quadrants and all 12 segments. An organization need no longer be defined by one stereotype. This reflects our conceptual framework where an integrated organization harnesses the strengths of all extremes and is not restricted to choosing between the extreme options.

By using cross-validating questions we have verified whether opposites and contradictions within one corporate culture have been reconciled. So, for example, we ask respondents to rate statements such as *"There is a clear and overt strategy for the future"* (Guided Missile) and *"Through our short-term thinking we are quick on our feet"* (Incubator). They are validated by a (combination of) reconciling statement such as *"We are able to meet short-term demands without compromizing our long-term vision"* (Reconciliation).

In older versions of this questionnaire we would have shown a scale between short- and long-term orientations. In this new reconciling framework we can score high or low on both! And a high score on both indicates a more powerful and higher performance culture.

Another example is the tension between task (Guided Missile) and people (Family) orientation, which we explore with the contrasting statements: *"There is a lot of team work"* and *"People strive for self-realization"* and the validating statement *"We have teams that consist of creative individuals."*

The OVP shows how healthy an organizational culture is by covering all 12 segments AND the reconciliation between those segments as shown in figure 2.8. External validation (i.e., against departmental or functional performance indictors) shows that higher scores on **all** segments and on the validating reconciliation questions correlate directly with higher long-term organizational performance.

Low performing organizations score low on all segments. Industry "followers" have an average score and "market leaders" score high on all segments because they have an integral culture that is able to reconcile all the contradictions in their business (see figure 2.9).

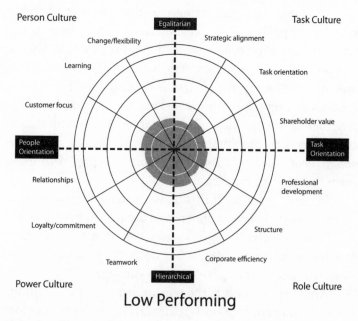

Low Performing

Figure 2.8 The Organizational Value Profiler 1 *(continued)*

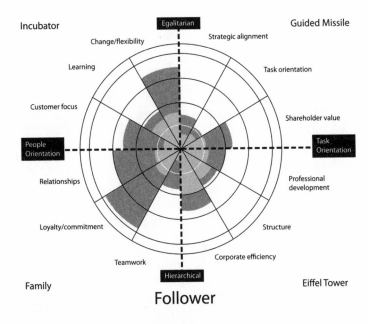

Figure 2.8 The Organizational Value Profiler 1 *(continued)*

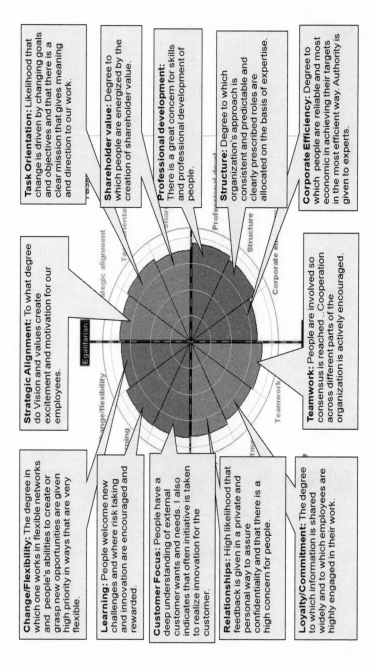

Task Orientation: Likelihood that change is driven by changing goals and objectives and that there is a clear mission that gives meaning and direction to our work.

Shareholder value: Degree to which people are energized by the creation of shareholder value.

Professional development: There is a great concern for skills and professional development of people.

Structure: Degree to which organization's approach is consistent and predictable and clearly prescribed roles are allocated on the basis of expertise.

Corporate Efficiency: Degree to which people are reliable and most economic in achieving their targets in the most efficient way. Authority is given to experts.

Strategic Alignment: To what degree do Vision and values create excitement and motivation for our employees.

Teamwork: People are involved so consensus is reached .. Cooperation across different parts of the organization is actively encouraged.

Change/Flexibility: The degree in which one works in flexible networks and people's abilities to create or grasp new opportunities are given high priority in ways that are very flexible.

Learning: People welcome new challenges and where risk taking and innovation are encouraged and rewarded.

Customer Focus: People have a deep understanding of external customer wants and needs. I also indicates that often initiative is taken to realize innovation for the customer.

Relationships: High likelihood that feedback is given in a private and personal way to assure confidentiality and that there is a high concern for people.

Loyalty/Commitment: The degree to which information is shared widely and to which employees are highly engaged in their work.

Figure 2.9 The Organizational Value Profiler 2

We can also explore "current" and "ideal" by asking respondents to give two sets of ratings for their own organization.

The value dilemmas that were selected from the interview and web-based processes are triangulated with the dilemmas identified by the OVP.

Linde—BOC measured on OVP

Let us take the example of the integration process of the German Linde AG and the British BOC Ltd. The top 150 leaders were asked to undertake a version of our internet driven OVP. The results were both revealing and insightful as is shown in figure 2.10.

Even at first glance the contrasts between BOC and the Linde Group legacy cultures are obvious. Legacy Linde is a German-based, highly professional organization with an excellent R&D division, centralized in its governance and highly successful after focusing on the gases and engineering business and divesting lots of unrelated businesses under a strong, visionary, and powerful leader, Dr. Wolfgang Reitzle. BOC was a highly successful global player with a multinational management team, rather project based, practical in its approach, and empowering people wherever possible, with a highly committed and loyal population.

Linde could be summarized as a highly professional, disciplined and mission oriented organization (a Guided-Eiffel Tower), and legacy BOC's strength was a combination of dedicated and empowered people around a clear set of global goals for the sake of shareholder value (a Guided-Family).

We derived the following key dilemmas from the OVP of the Linde Group:

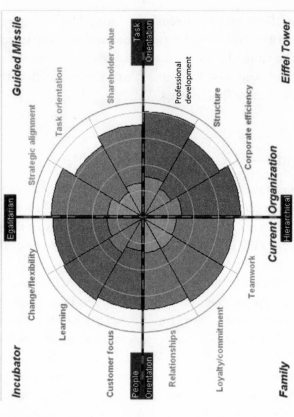

"Ideal" Organization for Future of the Linde Group (as described by participants)

- Less cultural inertia

- More integration and connections between values

- BOC and Linde described the same "ideal" future organization

- Larger differences between BOC legacy and "ideal" than Linde Legacy and "ideal"

Figure 2.10 Linde-BOC measured on OVP

1 We need to cut costs wherever we can for the sake of our shareholder's return vs. We need to invest for long-term sustainability.

2 We need to supply (global or standardized) products/services vs. We need to supply products/services that respond to local tastes and needs.

3 We need to develop our people vs. We need to keep people focused on delivering results.

4 We need to focus on the human element and take advantage of the experience of managing diversity vs. We need to enhance our culture of leading-edge engineering autonomy.

5 We need to develop looser controls and greater management empowerment vs. We need to develop tight top down controls and more restricted procedures.

6 Our leadership style should be more participative and empowering vs. Our leadership style should be more decisive and directive.

Dilemmas 3 to 6 were clearly value dilemmas; the success of the future Linde Group would be highly dependent on their reconciliations.

Norican Group—The Merger of Wheelabrator and DISA

Another example is the integration of Wheelabrator and DISA, two market leaders each with 100 years of operating history. DISA Group, the world's leading supplier of vertical molding, sand and core technologies, merged with Wheelabrator Group, the world's leading provider of metallic surface preparation equipment, spare parts and services. The two companies, both owned by Mid Europa Partners,

*were given official approval by the German Bundeskartel-
lamt to complete their merger process in April 2009.*

*As a united organization, DISA Group and Wheela-
brator Group employ 2,500 people across five continents
and together serve such diverse industries as aerospace,
automotive, energy, foundry, medical components, rail, and
marine. Following an internal competition within DISA
and Wheelabrator, a new name was chosen for the parent
organization: Norican Group. Robert E. Joyce Jr., president
and CEO of the newly merged company, said:*

> *This is an incredibly exciting time for the company, our
> employees, and our customers. I am confident that the
> creation of the Norican Group through the merger of
> DISA and Wheelabrator will provide our customers
> with world-class technologies and local service offers
> unparalleled in our industry. . . . In preparation for the
> merger, the management teams from DISA and Whee-
> labrator have been working together to combine the
> best of both companies. "Best of Both" became a theme
> during the planning process, and now it becomes reality
> as the result of all the planning comes to fruition.*

*It is in this spirit that we were invited to contribute. We had
a head start because the leaders believed in synergies which
were already reflected in the adoption of a new name.*

*The "Best of Both" program started with one of our
corporate culture scans supported by measurement on our
seven cultural dimensions. These scans supported, reinforced and validated the major dilemmas that came to the
surface as shown in figure 2.11.*

*The DISA culture was seen as more of a role-based Eif-
fel Tower with the risk that striving for perfection leads to
deadlines being missed. Moreover, change is realized within*

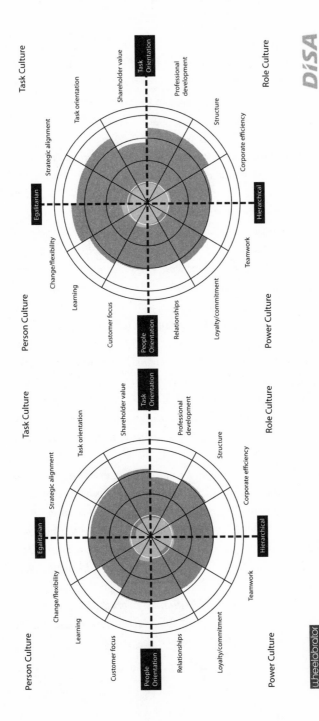

Figure 2.11 Wheelabrator DISA OVP

the core processes, rules and regulations. As a weak point, short-term thinking often compromises DISA's long-term vision. A strong point is that DISA's teams consist of creative individuals, reconciling the loyalty/commitment segment with the change/flexibility one.

Conversely, in the more shareholder driven culture of Wheelabrator, managers/executives at all levels understand and endorse the mission and objectives, and there is a clear and overt strategy for the future. People are results and achievement-orientated and are committed to getting the job done. In Wheelabrator the skills and capabilities of people are viewed as an important source of competitive advantage.

As in most international M&As we also used an additional instrument we call our Intercultural Assessment Profile (IAP). This enables participants to perform a comprehensive personal analysis of their own cross-cultural orientation. It uses the Seven Dimensions of Culture model developed by Trompenaars Hampden-Turner over a 15-year period. Some 80,000 managers have completed this questionnaire. A range of diagnostic questions is used to identify personal cross-cultural orientations against the reference model.

The primary aim is to help managers structure their experiences in order to facilitate rapid personal development for working in international business and/or integration situations. The IAP gives substance to the deeper national cultural arena in which international mergers are embedded.

Using this toolset, the following value dilemmas were brought to the fore:

- *We need to ensure that quality meets the high standards that clients expect vs. We need to move into developing markets to sell to the rest of the world.*

- We want to control our costs to deliver on our targets vs. We want to be a highly skilled technical company known for meeting all customer needs.

These first two dilemmas were cross-validated by the universalism-particularism score between the legacy companies and confirmed the nature of the dilemmas:

- Co-management to stimulate creativity and innovation vs. One manager to be fully responsible and streamline decision making.

The third dilemma was cross-validated by the higher individualistic score of Wheelabrator compared to DISA:

- We want to control costs to meet the objective of selling the company vs. We want to develop our people for future growth and sustainability.

The fourth dilemma was confirmed by our specific (cost-reduction) and diffuse (developing people) continuum:

- We need to develop our participative style (listening and reacting skills) vs. We need to develop better broadcasting and decision making (decisiveness).

Here the dimension of achievement and ascription was dominant, whilst for the sixth dilemma it was the time dimension that validated its existence:

- We need to focus on short-term goals to meet the objectives of the financiers and keep people motivated vs. We need to keep our attention on the long-term goals to ensure a sustainable organization which will be attractive to a buyer.

Once the dilemmas are formulated and validated by the difference in corporate and possibly other relevant cultures it is time to see how the personal values of the top leadership of the respective organizations can help in reconciling the dilemmas at stake.

> *This process begins by profiling the personal values of the leadership group and getting their commitment to value and behavioral change.*

Measurements: The Personal Values Profiler (PVP)

We use our Personal Values Profiler (PVP) when assessing the personal values of key players. There are no right or wrong answers and no orientation to any particular value is better or worse, but it offers important insights into the relationships that employees have with their organization. People from different cultures or professions will have different perspectives and will wish to pursue and prioritize their own interests, which are not necessarily the same as those of others.

A variant of our PVP is our CVP (Corporate Values Profiler). This is essentially the same tool but respondents are asked to indicate what values *should* drive the organization.

Unity on what matters for the individual and what matters for the organization is increasingly important. Imagine a young woman who has chosen a medical career because she perceives this to be congruent with her personal values (PVP profile). However, she finds that the reality of working in a publicly funded, city center hospital involves being verbally and physically abused by alcoholics and drug addicts and a focus on monitoring her work for the risk of being sued for any practice which doesn't accord with strict (Eiffel Tower) guidelines. The need for efficiency and conforming to procedure would be reflected in the hospital CVP and would be quite different from her PVP. Her response might be low motivation and performance, or to leave and work for a private health clinic that would be a closer match to her PVP.

In the case of Wheelabrator and DISA the (mean) PVP (Personal Value Profiles) are shown in figure 2.12.

Organizational Culture Profile That Reflects Personal Values of Respondents

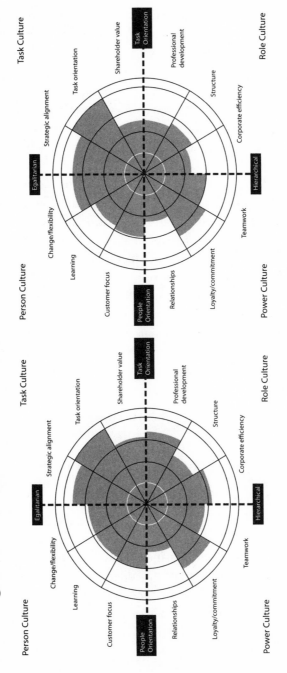

Figure 2.12 Wheelabrator DISA PVP

Exploring how the individual gives priority to different values and how these differ from other employees across an organization offers important insights into the relationships employees have with their organization. In the particular case of Wheelabrator and DISA it is surprising how similar the profiles are. There is perhaps a need for a little more change and flexibility at DISA and a bit more professional development and efficiency in the Wheelabrator leadership.

The PVP provides an understanding of matters concerning resistance or support for change and the capacity for stability, sustainability and innovation. These can exert a decisive influence on the overall ability of the organization to deal with the challenges and dilemmas it faces.

This PVP/CVP combination is usually cross-linked to our OVP (Organization Values Profiler) to provide additional important comparisons to corporate culture. We need to be alert for any mismatch between the values that will support the key purpose of NEWCO and the PVPs of key players.

Step 4: Choose values and behavior

Core values are instrumental in the achievement of the organizational goals and need to fit into the key purpose.

There are a variety of approaches to selecting the core values, including:

- Conceiving values as integral verbs;
- Values as helping key business dilemmas to be reconciled;
- Values as helping key cultural dilemmas to be reconciled;
- Values as giving life to purpose and mission;
- Values as extensions of personal values.

The necessity of "core values"

Values are fed by success and are vital in supporting the dilemma reconciliation process. So the best method for determining the core values is to end the process of reconciling the business dilemmas with the question:

What values and behaviors do we need to reconcile this dilemma and support its outcomes?

Some of the examples given below are very telling. In each case they followed the identification of the reconciliations for the most significant business dilemmas. An example from UniCredit may illuminate the importance of the selection of core values.

Groups of five to six people, including a range of representatives from across the organizations involved, were invited to consider one of the specific business dilemmas that had been generated. They worked through the six steps as described above and were then invited to describe which value(s) and behavior(s) needed to be developed to support the reconciliation of the dilemma. The first six steps of the dilemma reconciliation process normally lead to a lot of discussion around content. The seventh step, which asks participants to think about the values and behaviors necessary to support the action plan for reconciling the dilemma, effectively invites people to link the business dilemmas to certain values and behaviors. The case of UniCredit is slightly different in that the core values had already been established by CEO Allessandro Profumo. But he wanted to check on their validity and reliability. Contributors were invited to propose which values and behaviors from the existing set would best help to reconcile the dilemmas. They were encouraged to derive a new (set of) value(s), if needed. Let's see where this led.

The result, shown in table 2.4, was known as the "Integrity Charter" at UniCredit.

The process led to a wonderful exercise in which all the participants of different nationalities felt engaged and taken seriously. The values, though defined by top management, suddenly came alive when participants were invited to validate them and translate them into actual behavior. As a consequence UniCredit's values became the distilled product of all the different banks and company cultures that have crossed its path over the years. Although different, these cultures share a continual awareness of market developments, an unfailing commitment to the growth of added value, corporate social responsibility, staff development and customer relationships. As such, the six "Foundations of Integrity" informed the behavior of UniCredit people in their dealings with all their counterparts, including institutional entities such as government authorities and public officials. We have continued to study the Integrity Charter and it is a most impressive document. It is easy to see why the values cited would be important to UniCredit for guiding the integration process. However, like nearly all moral statements it contained omissions. It was not wrong. It was much better than most, yet it was incomplete. It would be better if the UniCredit values were balanced by their opposites.

Fairness, respect, reciprocity, transparency, trust and freedom are all nouns. At school we were taught that "a noun is a person, place or thing," although it can be an abstract idea. Since values are clearly *not* persons, places or physical things, they must be abstract ideas. If, say, trust is good, then "more trust" is better, so values can accumulate like money in a bank. It is at this point that our values tend to collapse beneath us! Thinking of values in contrasting

Table 2.4 The UniCredit Integrity Charter

Dilemma	Values	Effective and supporting behaviors
Shared commitment: Centralized vs. Decentralized Excellence	reciprocity, transparency, trust	Alignment of the businesses by sharing best practices, improve communication on existing governance and processes
Transnational Team: Italian vs. Other European cultural traits	freedom, trust	Defining processes for talent development and recruiting consistent with key competencies, develop process to complement team diversity
Communication success story: "AWARD" for champions managing diversity Meetings: Ante-chambering vs. Equal opportunities to contribute	respect transparency, trust	Golden rules for meetings, where accountability is clarified and leaders walk the talk
First Mover: Independence vs. Accountability	reciprocity	Clear rules, standards and defined objectives, develop perimeter of competencies and link to remuneration system
Walk Your Talk: Proclaimed values vs. Opportunistic behavior	fairness	Develop people evaluation system, measurement of customer/people satisfaction, wide internal communication and emphasis on reputational risk
Communication: Subtlety vs. Communicability	respect, accountability, transparency	Group meeting architecture with clearer rules on presentations and show discipline/consistency
Code UniCredit: Entrepreneurial flair vs. Clear codification	freedom, transparency, fairness	Make heroes and visibly reward people, develop best practice sharing forums, reward sharing and distributing innovative ideas, and allow for failures

pairs offers additional insights because values become "differences," not "abstract things."

Arthur Anderson placed a huge amount of trust in Enron and ceased to exist as a consequence. Why? Because AA's job was not just to trust but to *verify through audits* that Enron was a trustworthy organization and *then* announce this to the world. Trust does not exist on its own but *has a relationship with* supervision. We learn to trust those we have frequently supervised, so we can trust them even more. Yes, trust *does* increase like money, but not alone. It must be joined to its opposite. Trust and supervision (or verification) grow together in integrity. We were intrigued to note that UniCredit were careful to apply their values to *relationships*. This we applaud, but they might try going one step further and apply these to *relationships between values espoused by different people*.

This same construct applies to all of the remaining values in their list.

Fairness and respect
Justice is the blind goddess, in both the Greek and Roman pantheons. She is blindfolded to prevent her seeing the personal attractiveness of the litigants so that she considers only the facts and the law. Were she to look upon the parties she would be unlikely to deem them equals.

In total contrast "respect" comes from Latin *respicere,* "to look at." You respect people when you look deeply into their souls. Of course in a hyper-culture, you would *both* treat people fairly *and* respect them deeply, but the tension between these values must be understood and managed. Everyone is entitled to equal treatment. When you treat people fairly, they will reveal more of themselves that you can come to respect.

Reciprocity and initiation
When people fail to reciprocate it is not usually because they are ungrateful, but because they did not feel that your actions towards them merited reciprocity. Presumably Uni-Credit wants people to *initiate* valued actions, not just repay them. The value of pairing reciprocity with initiation is that those who do not reciprocate can be urged to explain the *circumstances in which they would do so*. What *would* make them grateful? An investment bank we know calls this "Managing your Boss." Why is he not managing to make you feel grateful for what he does? What more could he do? If you do not want to reciprocate, at least say why! All of us have a responsibility to try to initiate better relationships of reciprocity.

Transparency and discretion
Transparency is an excellent value with a role to play in giving business units as much independence as possible. But like all values it needs a little qualification to make it really effective. Banking is a business where privacy and confidentiality are very important. Private banking customers don't want their wealth advertised. There are regions in Europe where financial mail is not even delivered to your home! We treat information about customers with discretion while being transparent about our own efforts to succeed. We open up our affairs but only to those whose business it is to know us better; otherwise information is private.

Freedom and responsibility
UniCredit's CEO, Allessandro Profumo, is *responsible* to shareholders. He can and does exercise many kinds of freedom in his business, all of which must help to discharge that responsibility or at least not impede it. He is "free to be responsible." He is *not* free to be irresponsible. This also

applies to those reporting to him. He gives them "intervals of freedom," a month or more free of his scrutiny, but for that time period they are responsible and the longer the period the *more* responsible they become. They have more freedom *but a greater responsibility for how they use it.*

Conceiving values as integral verbs

The example of UniCredit typifies one approach to finding the core values—that of asking what values would be most helpful in reconciling the business dilemmas. There are alternative scenarios where it may be more appropriate to follow a more inductive process where management is asked to develop values that would help them.

Let's recall the *"Beauty"* case where the consultants were building a new organization, PIOL. The end results were amazing. Let's first reflect on what were seen as the major dilemmas of PI and OL joining:

- The push of cutting edge products and unique services vs. The pull of scalable and reliable ongoing services and diagnostics.
- The offering of globally significant services to an international clientele vs. The offering of a solid Dutch service to intimate clients.
- The nurturing of creative individuals vs. The development of ever better team work.
- The continuous development of people vs. The contributions for shareholders.

When the participants were looking for values that could help to resolve these dilemmas, they initially found that all the suggestions were most beneficial to only one of the two organizations. So when *client-orientation* was raised as a possible value, two questions were asked: "Does it have to be a noun?" and, "What about our cutting edge services, the concepts that clients do not yet understand?" Similarly, the value of *teamwork* was highly criticized because some consultants were concerned that it would jeopardize the need for autonomous creativity. And what about *shareholder value*? Are shareholders coming first yet again? Interestingly, the PI consultants, who were used to investing at least 25% of total turnover in R&D, better understood the need for this value, because in tough times, no compromise had been made in continuing the R&D effort, even in cases where this led to losses. They felt this was unsustainable. This became even clearer in their interactions with the OL consultants who were used to lower R&D investments and higher shareholder dividends What to do to connect these different points of view?

However, after further discussion, they clearly understood that for values to be effective and functional, they needed to be integrated with their opposite, as we described above. The process of describing values that was undertaken at UniCredit was replicated by PIOL. They ended up including the following:

- Striving for teamwork that consists of creative individuals;
- Striving for local learning so that it can be rolled out globally;
- Striving to continuously develop leading edge products and services that serve client needs;
- Striving to develop shareholder value to further develop people.

These values are integrative, and from here on, lots of attention needs to given to how to make this new mindset a reality. What behaviors need to be displayed to confirm that these values are being lived in all sincerity? This implementation is discussed later when we explore the "values to behavior" sessions and the key performance indicators (KPIs) that form the basis of monitoring take up.

Values as an aid to reconciling key cultural dilemmas

It really is satisfying to see parties engaging around a shared reality that they want to create together rather than focusing on differences. However, we can't overlook the risk of potential value clashes on the path to achieving that shared reality. A similar approach to that taken in reconciling business dilemmas can be used in reconciling cultural dilemmas.

In the case of UniCredit, clashes between "typically" Italian and German orientations came to the fore, which were confirmed in the findings of our OVP diagnostic scores. It was obvious that if these challenges were not overcome, whilst respecting the strengths of both approaches, the performance of NEWCO would suffer.

The first dilemma we framed focused on the problems of creating a new pan-European culture:

> *The new UniCredit Group is committed to co-creating a European hyper-culture and building up the future leadership from individuals with valuable cross-border experience.*
>
> **But** *this strategy faces strong counter forces from the teams in different countries. Local "old-boy networks" hint that re-integration into regional teams will be hindered by accepting international assignments.*

The reconciliation of this dilemma (shown in figure 2.13) was crucial in enabling the future effectiveness of UniCredit. The new management teams suggested the following:

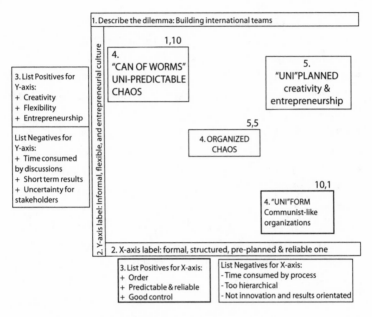

Figure 2.13 Unicredit transnational working dilemma

- Create a European-wide "talent program."
- Identify and develop talents systematically with fast-track programs.
- Create cross-boundary opportunities for the best talents.
- Formulate attractive expatriate policies.
- Incentivize international assignments and expatriation.
- Formulate fair and attractive re-integration policies.
- Concentrate European-wide function for expatriate career development at headquarters.
- Develop and implement promotion and job posting policies which explicitly favor talent with international assignment experience.
- Explore dual incumbency with leaders from across boundaries.
- Support internal networking of talents.

- Offer internet based communication tools.
- Encourage bank-wide network directories, personal yellow pages, etc.
- Attract external hires with the opportunities and projects that only the "first truly European Bank" can offer.
- Bonus programs to incentivize both own and cross boundary cooperation success.
- Create blog-like communication tools and peer group networking to help foster communities and bridge distance.
- Make networking for all employees a key to better cooperation across boundaries in the bank.
- Conduct regular face to face meetings of sufficient frequency and length to foster development of personal rapport and trust.

The second dilemma was about the different ways meetings are held and decisions made:

> *The Italian executives reach decisions by ante-chambering before meetings and the non-Italians often feel excluded from this very subtle and intimate decision-making culture. Italian executives expect meetings to maintain the pre-decision consensus.*
>
> *The Austrian and German executives prepare for meetings with agendas and detailed documents distributed to participants for pre-meeting consideration. They expect to discuss the decision options <u>during</u> meetings and for agreement to be reached <u>in</u> meeting.*

Many comments were added about the post-meeting implementation process. Italian executives expect decisions to leave them a degree of freedom in implementation. Austrian and German executives want clear decisions with specific well-defined actions. Germans will institute the solutions whilst Austrians will instead find another solution they like more and implement that!

This dilemma was mapped as shown in figure 2.14 by some selected groups.

Further follow-up meetings with the initial 60 interviewees led to reconciliations within the following actions:

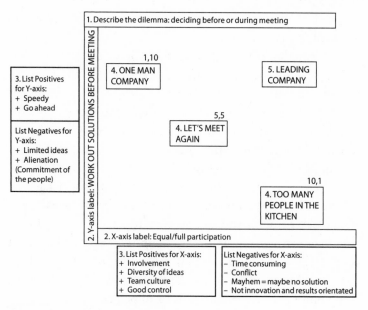

Figure 2.14 Unicredit meeting culture dilemma map

- Find volunteers who are willing to make the implicit communication rules explicit for each culture.
- Propose a reconciliation of styles that improves the speed and quality of decision making and then have the management committee modify and approve it.
- Communicate the results.
- Create learning opportunities to acquire the skills for communicating in the cross-cultural communication style.
- Access local support offered by co-facilitators from different cultures.

Another example of how the success of an organization depends upon the reconciliation of different value orientations is provided by the leadership principle upon which the legacy Linde and BOC cultures based their delegation and accountability.

Through our OVP diagnostic we had found that Linde was a typically German "Eiffel Tower" culture that embodied the principle: *"Vertrauen ist Gut aber Kontrolle ist besser,"* an expression often attributed to Lenin. On the other hand the "Guided Missile" culture of BOC was generally led through delegation and management by objectives. Obviously both orientations (top-down and bottom-up) had their advantages and disadvantages as shown in the following dilemma illustrated with cartoons in figure 2.15.

Working with this at the very top level of the Linde organization led to the value *"empowering people."* But look at the additional text that was added to this attractive value. It shows they really understand that a value is not a thing but a process in search of its opposite.

It is best captured by the supporting text: "People are given the space to contribute and grow."

Why this value?

Dilemma – Top-Down versus Bottom-Up

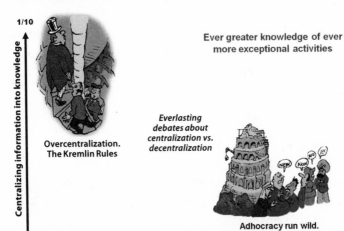

Figure 2.15 Linde BOC cultures dilemma

- Our people create our success.
- We believe that capable and responsible people can make a difference.
- We trust our people and believe in empowering individuals and teams to do the right thing.

Key supporting values:

- Accountability, trust and transparency.

Behaviors:

- We agree to clear goals and hold people accountable.
- We define boundaries but give people space for taking the initiative, learning and personal fulfillment.
- We encourage entrepreneurship.
- We stand up for what we believe in and do the right thing.

- We support the development of people and coach people for success.
- We each personally behave in ways consistent with our foundational principles of safety, integrity, sustainability and respect.

We reject:

- Bullying, fear and micromanaging.

So, for Linde, empowering comes with accountability—trust with clear goals. That makes it integrative and it works very well in this highly successful organization.

Values giving life to purpose and mission

Having checked their values against their vision and founding principles, the Linde Group CEO, Dr Reitzle, said:

> *September 6, 2006, marked the beginning of a new era for our company: the birth of the Linde Group. The merger of Linde and BOC created a leading global gases and engineering player with a strong position in all markets and core areas of expertise worldwide. . . .*
>
> *We have the ability to make even greater differences to the world through innovative solutions in areas such as clean energy, energy efficiency, safer and healthier food processing and distribution, waste-water treatment, environmental protection and health care. We will be relentless in our search for new technologies, applications and services in these and other areas for the benefit of mankind and our planet. . . .*

Our vision gives us identity about what we are as a group, and focuses our energy on the direction that we move in and what we want to achieve.

Our core values and foundational principles provide a framework that helps to guide our decisions and actions. They influence the way we behave and interact with one another. They guide the way we deal with customers. They set standards for engaging with other stakeholders. They affect the way we are viewed, as individuals and groups, both inside and outside the organization.

Many hundreds of employees have had the opportunity to participate in the identification of our core values and foundational principles. Many different views and perspectives have emerged; however, there have been some core key values that people have consistently agreed and identified with. Linde people around the world agree that these are the values and principles we should all live by.

Organizational values as extensions of personal values

In some cases the original organizations have so many different histories and so many vested interests that it is best to work from a clean slate. Rather then brainstorming about what existing values would best fit the NEWCO, we often advise the joint top leadership to respond to our Personal Value Profiler. The PVP elicits the personal values of the leadership and compares them to an initial set of values they individually believe are appropriate for the organization. Ideally there should be a match between the two of course—and there usually is. Presumably that is why they are with the organization in the first place!

In this way the PVP validates the OVP and the core values that are defined. In some cases it is most effective to begin with the leader's values and work from there. An example of this approach is provided in our work with the Campofrío Group. In the beginning the group had consisted of many independently operating organizations across Europe. They began to define top down what their values should be:

> *Our defining values as a company will revolve on a winning culture that is based on:*

- *Our **quick** responsiveness to customers' and consumers' needs.*
- *Our adherence to quality and trustworthiness.*
- *Our being focused on **action and speed**.*

It was quite clear that people felt uncomfortable at the first joint meeting of country heads with the European management team. Firstly it was just the very top management that had defined the core values, and secondly they were seen as too generic. Despite that, they played an important role in stimulating further discussion.

The responses we obtained from our PVP showed the rank-order of personal values, as shown in table 2.5.

We clustered these according to the OVP as a means of deriving some conceptual structure. It was positive to see that the values were nicely distributed across the 12 segments of our extended corporate culture OVP model. So customer-orientation, flexibility, open-mindedness and entrepreneuship loaded the three segments of the "Incubator." Reliability, consistency and efficiency loaded the "Eiffel Tower" segments. Decisiveness, focus, performance, achievement and result orientation were helping the "Guided Missile" to get going and, finally, trust, commit-

Table 2.5 Campofrío PVP results

Customer-oriented	9
Reliable	7
Flexibile	6
Decisive	5
Efficient	5
Entrepeneurial	5
Performance driven	5
Risk-taking	5
Achievement	4
Innovative	4
Result-oriented	4
Trusting	4
Open minded	3
Straightforward	3
Committed	2
Consistent	2
Encouraging	2
Energetic	2
Focused	2
Loyal	2
Team-oriented	2
Transparent	2

ment, team-orientation and loyalty suited the three segments of the "Family Culture."

From this point we discussed what values would best summarize the essence of the NEWCO, reconciling the business dilemmas and the personal values of its leadership. Gradually, the following credo was agreed on.

> **Commitment** *sustained with passion and talent allows us to deliver the best of ourselves and command the respect of all of our stakeholders. Commitment is demonstrated day to day in each decision and each action creating an environment that fosters achievement. Commitment is an atti-*

tude that guides us and allows us to responsibly fulfill our role in the company. Commitment is the cornerstone of our success.

Relationships *are the foundation of our business. Relationships with each and every one of our stakeholders and the community at large are built over time and are our most valuable asset. Relationships that are respectful and sincere drive loyalty to our company by consumers, clients, suppliers and employees. Relationships and teamwork that build on each partner's strengths are paramount for creating new opportunities to improve our business and sustain growth.*

Entrepreneurship *at all levels will make us more creative, quicker off the mark, and bolder. Entrepreneurship means taking initiatives in the relentless pursuit of excellence while respecting the established corporate objectives. Entrepreneurship is expected from each member of the company and provides us with first-to-market opportunities that energize our reputation and inspire the industry. Entrepreneurship is an attitude that defies the status quo and when large corporations act like small businesses the returns are immeasurable.*

Diversity *leads to creativity and the development of groundbreaking ideas. Diversity is a treasure that should be nurtured and leveraged in every discipline to accommodate different viewpoints and practices. Diversity allows us to think outside of the box and to select and implement the ideas that will provide us with a competitive edge and sus-*

tained growth over time. Diversity gives employ-
ees ownership of our successes. Diversity drives
leadership.

One team, one vision, one mission

The end result was very inclusive and reflected all the
participants reconciling business and personal needs. The
discussion centerd on what the new Campofrío Group was
sharing rather than all the differences that made up the
organization from the outset.

Exploring the core values of the organization through metaphors

We sometimes use metaphors to explore an organization's
core values. In this process we ask leaders and managers to
think about their organization and then name a car brand,
an animal, a football team and/or a movie star that in some
way encapsulates or reflects the essence of the company. In
fact we ask them about metaphors that describe both the
current state of their (legacy) organization and metaphors
that describe the ideal state once they have merged.

An example outcome of this exercise is presented in
figure 2.16, concerning the merging of a French and a Dutch
organization.

Metaphors suggest different PATTERNS of RELA-
TIONSHIPS. The beauty of metaphors in this methodology is that they stimulate the participants to detach from
their current reality and come up with a coherent analogue.
This approach enables people to conceptualize issues in a
risk-free and depersonalized format and provides valuable
insights into what people are thinking and what they believe
(figure 2.17 on page 97).

Corporate Identity—Car Metaphor

Current	Ideal	Why?
Audi A5	Volvo XC 90	I think in general we are quite well equipped for our task. Work with dedicated teams and do have good teams in general
Volvo	Toyota	Safe, structurally sound, boring and not very trendy, slow to react, i.e., like a tank
A bus	a four wheel car	With a lot of different people in it, having different destinations
Renault	some Japanese brand (don't ask which one, I'm a woman ;))	Pretty national, somehow traditional brand
Toyota on gasoline	hybrid Toyota	Mass brand which appeals to a lot of people. Good quality sometimes perceived as too expensive (hence gasoline)
Logane	Toyota Prius (hybrid)	Good value for money—acceptable quality for low cost. Diversified range of products—optimize and simplify the requirements.

Figure 2.16 Metaphors 1

A metaphor has been defined as the LIKENESS of UNLIKE characteristics. Hence SNOW is LIKE a blanket. Snow is also UNLIKE a blanket.

The word comes from meta, meaning "above" and phor, meaning "description." Hence, it is "above descriptions." We can think of it as a BRIDGE between, for instance, STRATEGY and our capacity to REFLECT on strategy. Metaphors can STAND IN for what you are trying to invent, e.g., aluminium cans stood in for Canon's disposable drums for home copiers. The team was holding beer cans in their hands as it occurred to them. A paint company, whose paint sheeted off smooth walls when dry, imagined themselves to be mountaineers on a vertical cliff face, hacking into the rock to get footholds.

Current Organization—Animal Metaphor

Animal	Description
Octopus	Intelligent species that survived in mutations over many, many years—but with a heavy head in the center controlling what its tentacles are doing.
Hippo	Big, robust, but a little sedate.
Antelope	Running around in panic, not really sure where to and why.
An octopus which grows from octo to nona or decapus or more and the arms are constantly moving	Diversity, agility, constant change.
(Fat) Elephant	Powerful, well known, respectable, solid, and robust institution.
Elephant with tiger mind	Solid, technical, a little bit slow, with good image and willing to be more aggressive.
A zoo? We are not one animal, we are many different types	We are still a collection of different organizations not yet quite integrated. However, there is also a great strength in our diversity (especially as we represent the diversity of our customers) if we can harness it.
A snake which is in the middle of the process of changing its skin	Changing the skin is a process linked to growing-up and to evolving to the "next stage." This process can take time, can even be painful and can, for the time it takes, slow down the ability to react to the challenges of the environment.

Ideal Organization

Animal	Description
A racehorse	Well focused, speed, passion to win.
Dolphin	Agile, flexible, fast, good orientation, good communication, living in groups but enough space for some individualism.
Lion	Powerful, fast and swift, but also lying in the sun, looking around, being calm and thoughtful, i.e., not active all the time, but when active, very focused.
Leopard	Out to win and profit on everything it does. Fast, successful hunter, adapts quickly to changing circumstances. Although not the biggest animal around very well respected by others. Works in win-win animal networks as well as alone.
Fox	Smart. Capable. Focus on the family. Highly adaptable. Willing to hunt.
A crossing of lions and termites	The organized hunting of lions in line with the high social skills and willingness to work of termites.
An eagle	Dominating the airspace, flying high but relaxed, always focused and ready to hit when the prey is worth the effort.
A hawk	The hawk can see targets from a long distance, and can move fast towards them. It can select its speed and altitude and easily overcome natural barriers. It does not have to fear natural enemies in its environment.

Figure 2.17 Metaphors 2

The organization of core values

Core values constitute a guiding value framework. Therefore, limiting the number of core values increases transparency and simplifies the creation of the "value driven organization." We generally suggest reducing the list to a maximum of four. Importantly, the core values will need translating into effective behavioral values (desired behavior). Subsequently they can be communicated and implemented in the day-to-day business, systems and processes.

We want to stress that there is no priority in these values—all are important to the daily running of the business, whether it is in a meeting, while making a leadership decision, while dealing with employees individually or in a group, even in dealing with vendors, customers, and shareholders. The selected core values need to be the underlying theme of all communication and action, encapsulating the company's cultural essence in support of the strategic business case.

Translating values into behaviors

Here we begin to translate values into day-to-day practice by identifying the behaviors that express and embody the values. This includes:

1 Giving direction to acceptable and unacceptable behaviors;
2 Imagining the future;
3 Making crucial decisions.

While the OVP, PVP and IAP focus on diagnosing the main **differences** between the key parties and individuals involved, this step focuses on what the newly created organization needs to **share**. It revisits the complete overview of the dilemmas that need to be addressed, both in terms of business and culture, in order to create a sustainable high performance culture in the post-merger process.

As we said earlier, the "value" of a "shared value" is in the degree to which it helps to reconcile the basic business and cultural dilemmas the organization is facing whilst integrating towards NEWCO.

So what does the combined organization consider to be of value? The definition of an organization's core values is based on what drives us and what binds us. Core values are the timeless tenets of an organization. Together with its key purpose it reflects what the organization stands for and tells this story to the outside world.

Process and tools for translating values into behaviors (V2B): "The Integrity Charter"

This is the process of defining desirable and undesirable behaviors. The end product can be expressed as a "Charter of Behavior." The objective is to improve common understanding, trust, communication, cooperation and effectiveness in a team. It also initiates actions in the team and individual team members that help in "living" the behaviors in the charter.

Two basic processes to define or fine-tune the core values of the newly established organization can be used:

1 It is important to have started with the leadership group and their direct reports in a dilemma reconciliation workshop in which the basic business and cultural dilemmas are reconciled through a series of parallel dilemma reconciliation processes (DRP) as described earlier. This allows us to begin selecting the shared values and behaviors that support the DRP.

2   After the first selection of shared (core) values has been made, a value-to-behavior (V2B) workshop needs to be run. Again, we begin with the leadership group (highest level of intact group). The Values to Behavior (V2B) process uses the organizations' core values to re-establish trust and improve communication within and between teams, thus improving daily cooperation and performance.

The process consists of several steps, beginning with the creation of a "Charter of Behavior" and ending with actions for better "living" these behaviors. The charter lists behaviors, desirable as well as undesirable, that the team considers key in the effective handling of the daily workload and the creation of a positive and constructive work environment.

Every core value is translated into desirable or undesirable behaviors using a facilitating structured worksheet. Teams discuss the individual statements, and then, again individually, the statements are ranked before a final phase of group evaluation. The whole process results in the selection of the most important core values for the leadership team, selection of desirable and undesirable behaviors for the team, and finally the production of a charter.

The following steps need to be followed:

- Select the first core value to "translate" and discuss barriers.
- Individual team members complete the worksheet by thinking of specific, concrete, observable behaviors. Thus, "being trustworthy" is not concrete enough. Ask how someone would **show** that they are trustworthy. Such as: "When you promise something, do it!"
- Be willing to illustrate the behaviors you desire with a recent example.
- Discuss what has been offered and share examples.

- Facilitator/scribe: capture what is being said on a flip chart.
- Select the second, third, fourth, etc. core value, address any barriers, and repeat the process.
- Prioritize the statements on the flip charts with colored stickers.
- Record with a photograph of the team.
- Create the Internal Charter of Behavior by collating the dominant statements per core value (desirable and undesirable behavior) as in the example in figure 2.18.
- Finally, practice what you preach by having a fun "Living the Charter" session!

But don't just put this in a filing cabinet or on a noticeboard. You need to bring it to life by:

- Connecting what is in the charter to the current business challenges.
- Deciding on cascade-down actions to subordinate teams so that everyone lives the charter.
- Deciding on candidates for external exchange sessions.
- Deciding on the needs for dilemma reconciliation and intervention.
- Deciding on a scheme for monitoring and measuring behavior improvement.
- Assessing leadership support requirements.
- Determining internal communication requirements.
- Identifying what other support/actions are needed to secure momentum.

V2B uses the energy released by values that are genuinely shared within the organization, such as the core values that capture what the organization stands for. Typically core values reflect what binds and connects those working for the organization and are part and parcel of the corporate

Internal Charter of Behavior

What the Members of the Management Board Expect from Each Other

SHARING *(to address the general lack of time and lack of support to prepare properly)*

Supporting values	Observable behavior	
	DESIRABLE: I want you to...	**UNDESIRABLE: I don't want you to...**
Transparency	1. Exchange opinions and values	1. Make promises you cannot keep
Openness	**2. Visibly enjoy work**	**2. Take things too personally**
Relevance	3. React to what I say	3. Make me believe that you can do everything at once
Clarity	4. Respect non-property people and show it	4. Act with no respect for the past
		5. Overwhelm me (leave me room)

PREDICTABLE *(to address the need for more trust)*

Supporting values	Observable behavior	
	DESIRABLE: I want you to...	**UNDESIRABLE: I don't want you to...**
Trust	1. Anticipate developments and share your vision	1. Tell different stories to different people
Responsible behavior	**2. Show respect for my solution by reacting; positively or negatively**	**2. Keep putting pressure on people**
Sense of humor	3. Be open in all aspects of the subject matter	3. Let yourself be taken by surprise
Accountability	4. "Live" a decision	4. Put the blame elsewhere
		5. Be complacent

TEAM PLAY *(to address differences in objectives and the need for respect)*

Supporting values	Observable behavior	
	DESIRABLE: I want you to...	**UNDESIRABLE: I don't want you to...**
Mutual Respect	1. State what you really think	1. Criticize team members
Assistance and help	**2. Support weaknesses and stimulate strengths**	2. Attack rather than reconcile
Inspired engagement	3. Be interested in me and show it	3. Keep your cards close to the chest
	4. Show empathy	
	5. Be relaxed	

IMPROVEMENT *(to address too much functionality—silo behavior—and "years of experience" mentality)*

Supporting values	Observable behavior	
	DESIRABLE: I want you to...	**UNDESIRABLE: I don't want you to...**
Creativity	1. Focus on high impact items	**1. Postpone tough decisions**
Pro-activity	2. Share networks	**2. Spend too much time on details**
Benchmarking	3. Develop a vision of where to go	3. Lose time on unrealistic deals
Creating win-wins	4. "Manage" two levels down	4. Hire consultants
	5. Coach your staff	

Figure 2.18 Sample Internal Charter of Behavior

identity. However, they often fail to energize management and employees. Why is this? The answer is because core values are often too abstract to give guidance in real life situations. Values need to be interpreted or translated for their relevance in daily work. This is what is happening in the V2B process, and this is why the charter is important in bringing it all to life.

V2B builds on the powerful centuries-old adage "Do unto others as you would have others do unto you." In a V2B workshop, participants explore the behavior they expect from each other. From this they then jointly create an Internal Charter capturing a limited number of observable desirable and undesirable behaviors for further embedding and "living."

Where cooperation between two teams needs improvement a so-called external V2B process is needed. Here both teams create an External Charter, capturing the behaviors each team expects from the other (e.g., suppliers or another department). After exchanging and explaining the External Charters, both teams will create an action program to better "live" the desirable behaviors.

Intact teams

This process is designed for intact teams (maximum recommended size 20) because it helps to operationalize the translation process into relevant behaviors that help the team perform better. An "intact team" can be defined as any group with common tasks and common culture at any level in the organization. Another reason for working through this V2B process with intact teams is that the team members can monitor whether the actual behaviors are indeed expressed. For example, it can be useful to have one member of the team checking the behavior within meetings and devoting some time at the end of the meeting to offering constructive feedback. Members can rotate this role.

A complex but wonderful example of how values that appear abstract can be translated into behaviors was worked through between the consultants of PI and OL. Recall that the core values that they agreed for PIOL were:

- Striving for teamwork that consists of creative individuals;
- Striving for local learning so that it can be rolled out globally;
- Striving to continuously develop leading edge products and services that serve client needs;
- Striving to develop shareholder value to further develop people.

We asked them the questions:

Q1 What could my colleague do that would lead me to truly and spontaneously say:
   "This is really a good example of . . . (e.g.) striving for teamwork that consists of creative individuals."
Q2 What should my colleague not do?
   "And what is the type of behavior you would not do for that same value?"
Q3 Can you illustrate your statement with examples?

Tables 2.6 through 2.9 show some examples of such a dialogue. We put all the ideas on paper and asked people to distribute three votes each (the scores clearly indicate the most popular suggestions).

Sessions for developing such charters typically take half a day including discussion on implementation, especially about how to monitor progress in the expression of behaviors. Individual team members can also be invited to suggest a particular behavior that they feel needs special attention. These programs are very successful and are easily extended and cascaded to support staff and mixed account teams for larger clients. For PIOL, the process led to a new focus on shared values and behaviors, and the legacy problems and past ineffective behaviors were soon left behind.

Table 2.6 Striving for teamwork that consists of creative individuals

+ Desirable I would like you to . . .		– Undesirable I do not want you to . . .	
Share my individual ideas with the team - Always go to clients with colleague - Paraphrase what others are saying to check understanding	4	Keep information for a few selected people only	1
Be proactive		Avoid responsibility	
Not agree on product innovations that are not "Orange"		Hide behind my back	
Bring solutions, not problems	4	Cover your back all the time	
Explore new solutions together		Make yourself bigger than the company	
Divergent thinking	1	Say "we cannot do it," "we tried it before, but it didn't work!"	4
Challenge each other constructively - Open positive communication	3	Focus on individual problems/small stuff	
Be persistent/Do not take "no" for an answer	4	Become complacent with individual success	
Do big thinks + think big		Take things for granted: delegate without checking	
Actively participate in an authentic way		Surround yourself with people who tell you what they think you would like to hear	7
Show guts and ask team to become safety net	1	Only raise problems without solutions	1
Be supportive of ideas		Follow each other like lemmings	1

Table 2.7 Striving for local learning so that it can be rolled out globally

+ Desirable I would like you to . . .		− Undesirable I do not want you to . . .	
Avoid unnecessary complication		Say "yes," think "no"	2
Share major problems, challenges and worries	5	Talk about dissatisfaction with everybody but me	
Be available to all, not just management and the press		Exhibit passive/hidden resistance	1
Communicate regularly and relentlessly to people outside your local team	6	Hide behind local policy	3
Invest time in people and building trust	4	Be sensitive to "brown-nosing"	3
Give the "flowers" to the others		Create barriers to access	3
Be fair in judgments about non-members of your direct team, even when they are negative		Misuse hierarchy/reliance on hierarchy as a filter	4
Proactively approach people		Practice politics	1
Solicit opinions/actively seek new ideas	3	Use only email communication to avoid dialogue	1
Check understanding by paraphrasing and opening up communication channels		Close your door (managing by walking around)	

Table 2.8 Striving to continuously develop leading edge products and services that serve client needs

+ Desirable I would like you to . . .		− Undesirable I do not want you to . . .	
Strive for excellent/quality performance every time and find out through feedback	1	Be sloppy	
Focus on solutions that delight the client		Find reasons/excuses that things won't work	3
First think then execute		Always have an excuse—blame!	5
Deliver what has been promised	2	Cover up mistakes (lack of ownership)	
Always think about client first		Not deliver what has been promised	
Co-produce as much as possible with client	9	Focus on short-term success to please client	2
Focus/maintain your aim		Slowly execute to be perfect	
Give actionable feedback		Avoid responsibility for the process or the idea	2
Be specific about expectations		Switch subjects	
Have sense of urgency, don't procrastinate or go for the perfect service		Disrespect feedback from client	1
Ask for a direct, honest explanation by client		Go for the quick buck	

Table 2.9 Striving to develop shareholder value to further develop people

+ Desirable I would like you to . . .		– Undesirable I do not want you to . . .	
Deliver on promises	3	Just learn without application	5
Take responsibility for own actions and income	1	Have a hidden agenda	
Talk openly and truthfully (walk the talk)	1	Find reasons/excuses for things going wrong	
Focus on customer needs <u>and</u> shareholders—start the "thinking" from the customer but make it profitable	8	Avoid issues	1
Learn to earn	4	Just learn individually without application	7
Develop new products with a business plan		Think only about the next quarterly results	
Experiment with new products	1	Have turnover for the sake of turnover	2
Be selective in the type of turnover (quality only)		Participate in gossip and rumor	2

Step 5: The business case for integration

This final step in Phase A is aimed at keeping everyone on course and moving in the same direction. At this stage the leadership team has enough information to develop a detailed implementation program.

- They have customized this communication so it aligns with the key drivers of the total population.
- They have a clear sense of collective direction, vision and mission.
- They know the core values, principles and (key) purpose.
- They have a set of behaviors and drivers that guide their day-to-day decision making and actions.

Before implementing a process of whole-system integration involving culture change, it is vital that the CEO and the Board have indentified and clarified the compelling reasons for the integration. A convincing link must be made between the performance issues and the cultural issues. The CEO and his or her team should present a clear story line so the reasons for the whole-system integration and change effort are clearly understood and supported by the executive and employee populations.

And this goes beyond just improving current performance; it is more about how they can position themselves to take advantage of value differences and build long-term resilience and sustainability.

In summary, after the previous steps, the following will have been made clear:

- A clearly defined joint visionary framework and purpose.
- The cultural and value differences and similarities on personal, team and organizational levels.

- The main business and cultural dilemmas that need to be reconciled.
- The main core values and behaviors that will enable the reconciliations to be successful.

These are all the ingredients necessary to develop the second phase of the implementation of NEWCO's strategy, the key objectives, and KPIs (key performance indicators).

PHASE B: DEVELOPING IMPLEMENTATION STRATEGY THROUGH OBJECTIVES AND KPIs

The focus now shifts to planning the implementation strategy and its key performance indicators (KPIs) in order to realize the business benefits of the merger/alliance. This second phase consists of two basic steps and begins to apply the results of the diagnosis and analysis undertaken in Phase A:

Step 6   Survey of key drivers

Step 7   Develop implementation through objectives and key performance indicators (KPIs)

Step 6: Survey of key drivers

Organizational identity renewal requires the reconciliation of divergent goals, values, and structural, functional and cultural differences. Our approach is to synthesize strategy, structure, operations, people, and culture into a single integrated whole which also includes the economic, social and cultural context in which the new organization functions. Taking the perspective of the company as a whole, we seek to identify how these elements can be aligned and reconciled to generate maximum performance.

It is necessary to validate the key drivers for the following reasons:

- To customize the design of the *communications* surrounding the integration process, particularly the compelling reason for change.
- To customize the methodology and content of the cultural integration process.
- To provide executives and managers with personal feedback for coaching purposes.

By validation, we mean that the drivers should be objectively assessed rather than simply assumed. But there is a motivation through participation aspect as well. We use the process of validating a key purpose and its core values to align all participants in the process.

Process and tools

It is important that the leadership team validates the BHAG (big, hairy, audacious goal) and fundamental reason for being or key purpose because this will give the core values a context. Because the "key purpose" needs to serve as a guiding star on the horizon, which the organization will ever pursue but never reach, it needs to be co-produced with the involvement of as many participants as possible, rather than just superimposed from the top. Purpose and values are what guide, inspire and give meaning to all the work being done within the integrated organization, so they need to come from all involved.

Once the key purpose statement has been drafted by the very top executives, it needs to be validated by the layers below. It should be easily understood and open to enrichment through constructive criticism.

As an example, Geodis Wilson proposed the following to its top 200 meeting:

> *Geodis Wilson is recognized as the best freight management service provider by customers, suppliers and employees.*

Your reaction: What is good?

Your reaction: What should be changed to improve the BHAG?

> *Deliver cutting edge integrated freight management solutions to our customers and excel in our care for information, innovation and consultation for them to be best in class.*

Your reaction: What is good?

Your reaction: What should be changed to improve the key purpose?

This led to a lively, highly participative and dynamic session in which people took ownership of the process.

Comparisons of the Organization Value Profiler (OVP) and Personal Values Profiler (PVP)

As explained earlier, the OVP provides an overview of both the current and ideal dominant values of the organization and maps the major differences between the organizations involved on those orientations. In contrast, the PVP gives an overview of the dominant personal values of the leadership of the organization. Tensions between these are a potential source of cultural inertia. In the modern workplace, it is essential to reconcile what matters for the organization and what matters for the employees.

Any such tensions must be analyzed and key drivers selected to close these gaps between current and ideal and between personal and organizational values. Cultural inertia needs to be reconciled at each level (leaders' personal values and organizational values) as well as between levels (what leaders value and what middle management values).

After this analysis the leadership must make a decision as to what the key drivers for the integration process are. These key drivers could be in functional areas like HR, marketing or even finance and the way these areas relate with each other.

Coaching of key players

It is important to connect key players in terms of their individual roles to the changes being promoted across the organization. In addition to more generic communication and participation in workshops and/or web-based activities, some selected key players may benefit from more personal counseling and coaching. Not only does this help them to sustain their own motivation and meet their goals, but it also contributes to the total change process through synergy. We use an approach based the ideas of Marshall Goldsmith and Pieter ter Kuile. Their method is as simple as it is powerful. Just ask people to reflect on what to stop, start, and continue in their behaviors.[1]

---

1   Goldsmith, M. "What got you here won't get you there," in *Stop en nu verder*, 2009.

Step 7: Develop implementation through objectives and key performance indicators (KPIs)

At this point the CEO and top leadership teams have sufficient information to develop a detailed implementation program. They have the compelling business reasons for the integration program; they have customized its communication and key drivers for the executive and employee population; they have a clear sense of collective direction—the vision, mission and purpose; they know the shared core values and behaviors to which they aspire; and they have a clear picture of where the parties currently are.

It is of vital importance to set targets for the integration process in performance, cultural and leadership improvements and capture them in a number of indicators. However, we go beyond "balanced scorecards" because, following the logic of our total process as described throughout this book, "balance" implies that if you have more of one, you have less of the other. That is not very fruitful when trying to get synergies between organizations. The benefit of reconciliation lies in integrating differences and connecting points of view. So we base performance indicators on our "integrated scorecard" in which we develop "key *reconciling* indicators" (KRIs) rather than simple KPIs. Monitoring change through KRIs takes the benefits of reconciliation right through to the final achievement of a hyper-culture and mindset change.

There are three types of indicators: "causal" indicators, "output" indicators that relate directly to performance, and "outcome" indicators that relate to end results.

"Causal" indicators

These are targets set for values and behavior improvement. Success would be reflected in a balanced OVP profile of NEWCO displaying a full complement of 12 segments showing that all the key dilemmas were reconciled leading to high performance. Similarly, measures at the individual level of the leadership would show improvement.

We often use the PVP and OVP for monitoring progress on the behavioral and value levels and do half-yearly scans to check for decrease in cultural inertia. The output of the V2B charters (as discussed in Step 5) are also taken as a reference point to see whether the intact teams and their individual members are making progress on "causal" indicators that relate to values and behaviors

On the individual level it is very important that the appraisal process reinforces the desired shared values and behaviors. It should be much more than just checking the completion of previously agreed-on deliverables as in conventional project management because this lacks the behavioral component.

In this process the superior should also check whether the individual has lived his or her corporate activities according to the espoused values and behaviors. In more comprehensive approaches this could be linked to the team feedback on how the V2B process has been lived by the individual.

In our *"Beauty"* case we observed that PIOL was stimulated in its integration process by introducing an integrated scorecard. How else can it be done if the values are to be integral? It all started with a workshop where the full organization of approximately 50 people gathered. The following process was initiated:

Recall their values:

- Striving for teamwork that consists of creative individuals;
- Striving for local learning so that it can be rolled out globally;
- Striving to continuously develop leading edge products and services that serve client needs;
- Striving to develop shareholder value to further develop people.

Assessing whether these values are being lived cannot be achieved using a method based on a linear scale. The following rhetorical questions, appropriate to the above values, serve to illustrate what needs to be assessed.

Question 1: What are the supporting values helping to reconcile teamwork-creative individuals?
Question 2: What are the key reconciling indicators that help us say: this is clear evidence for progress?
Question 3: What are the key behaviors that can help us say: this is clear evidence for this value?

Looking at the second question:
First, what is a key reconciling indicator? It is a behavioral output that indicates that you have lived the value. And it can't be specific enough; if possible it should be quantifiable or at least benchmarked. For example, on the first value a KRI was based on their invoices:

- What is the percentage of your individual contributions on all invoices now compared to other consultants on the team? And what will it be next year?

And one on information sharing indicators:

- How many times have you given internal seminars/ joint presentations to other consultants so they can take advantage of your newly developed materials?

On the local-global orientation the following KRIs were formulated:

- How many concrete examples can you give where a best consulting practice was communicated and used in the global network?
- What global offerings have you applied in the local market and how?

On the push and pull dilemma, the following KRIs were designed:

- What concrete examples of co-developed services with the client can you report?
- How many times were you asked for straight feedback by the client and adapted the service accordingly?

On shareholder value versus developing people, the following suggestions were adopted:

- What concrete and specific examples are there where the learning process has led to an actual increase in turnover and therefore profitability?
- What consulting or training processes were used to develop junior consultants?

The benefit of this approach lies in integrating the strengths of the different PI and OL consultants to create joint success. After the workshop, the process was installed on our web server to provide online access for the individual use of consultants and their superiors. The screenshots shown in figures 2.19 and 2.20 tell the story.

In this first screenshot we see that the individual consultant can score himself or herself on a dilemma grid, indicating previous (lower left) and current (upper right) positions.

The next screenshot shows how the key measures (or KRIs) are stored in an online database for retrieval at a later stage to check progress. This internet supported process provides the scope to update the KRIs and also indicates how the organizational leadership can help in making progress.

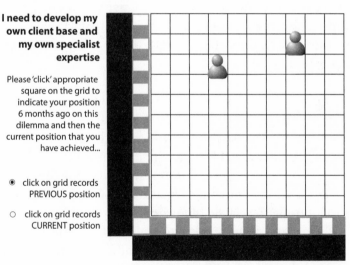

I need to develop my own client base and my own specialist expertise

Please 'click' appropriate square on the grid to indicate your position 6 months ago on this dilemma and then the current position that you have achieved...

◉ click on grid records PREVIOUS position

○ click on grid records CURRENT position

I need to share my knowledge and experiences of my clients and learning with others

Figure 2.19 PIOL workshop 1

Q1. In the form, under Key Reconciling Indicators, indicate the three key measures you had set yourself 6 months ago as evidence for the progress you had intended with this dilemma. Then describe the actual progress that you have made on each in the last 6 months (and/or the difficulties/problems you had that constrained your progress/development).

Key Reconciling Indicators (as previously conceived by you)	Evidence of Progress (and/or problems)
KRI 1:	
KRI 2:	
KRI 3:	

Figure 2.20 PIOL workshop 2

"Output" indicators

We define output targets as indicators of performance improvement in areas such as productivity, efficiency, innovation, and employee and customer satisfaction. These measures need to be aligned with the ongoing monitoring in the organization.

Adaptors versus Innovators: a way to integrate

When a large US-based pharmaceutical firm bought a much smaller Danish pharmaceutical outlet predominantly because of their highly innovative culture the US buyer insisted on pure interventions in the development of staff professional attitude competencies. The US firm had experience of using the classic Innovator-Adaptor style inventory of Kirton, and we were asked to build on that positive experience and see whether there were significant Kirton profiles amongst Danish and American professionals.

Kirton's KAI[2] measures individual styles of problem definition and solving. Style, in this case, refers to an adap-

---

2 Kirton, M.J. (ed.) *Adaptors and Innovators: styles of creativity and problem solving*, New York: Routledge, 1994.

tive, building or analogic problem-solving style versus an innovative or pioneering style. Jack Hipple's summary of the two groups, and how each group is viewed by its opposites, is shown in table 2.10.[3]

Kirton noted that some professionals were able to initiate change that improved the current system, but were unable to identify opportunities *outside* the framework of the system.[4] Kirton calls this style "adaptive." Other manag-

Table 2.10 Characteristics of Adaptors and Innovators

Adaptor	Innovator
Efficient, thorough, adaptable, methodical, organized, precise, reliable, dependable	Ingenious, original, independent, unconventional
Accepts problem definition	Challenges problem definition
Does things better	Does things differently
Concerned with resolving problems rather than finding them	Discovers problems and avenues for their solutions
Seeks solutions to problems in tried and understood ways	Manipulates problems by questioning existing assumptions
Reduces problems by improvement and greater efficiency, while aiming at continuity and stability	Is a catalyst in unsettled groups, irreverent of their consensual views
Seems impervious to boredom; able to maintain high accuracy in long spells of detailed work	Capable of routine work (system maintenance) for only short bursts; quick to delegate routine tasks
Is an authority within established structures	Tends to take control in unstructured situations

3 Hipple, J., et al. "Can corporate innovation champions survive?" *Chemical Innovation Magazine*, November 2001, vol. 31, no. 11, pp. 14–22.
4 Kirton, M.J. *Management Initiative*, London: Acton Society Trust, 1961.

ers were good at generating ideas to lead to more radical change, but failed to get their radical ideas accepted. Kirton termed this style "innovative." These observations gave rise to Kirton's hypothesis that there is a personality continuum called adaptor-innovator, which offers two very different approaches to change.[5]

The main weakness of Kirton's assumptions perhaps lies in their very succinctness and precision. One of the main assumptions is that cognitive style, which underlies the KAI instrument, is conceptually independent of cognitive capacity, success, cognitive techniques and coping behavior. We agree with this—but this all comes from an assumption that Kirton makes more implicitly: that the adaptor style and the innovator style are *mutually exclusive*. This is confirmed by the presentation of the scores of the classic KAI instrument as the scores on a *balance*, where a higher score on the adaptor side automatically results in a lower score on the innovator side.[6] Much as with the Meyers-Briggs Type Indicator (MBTI) the main focus is on the *preferences* that people have.

We asked some 250 managers from a variety of cultural backgrounds (but predominantly American and Danish) to complete our Integrated Type Indicator (ITI), which is a dual axis extension to the classic MBTI. Thus we explore, for example, how well a respondent can think as well as feel, not whether he or she thinks OR feels. In the same way, we extended the logic to produce a more complete version of the classic Kirton KAI.

We found that creative people move more effectively *between* intuition and thinking, that innovators extrovertly publish their introverted calculations and constantly learn by oscillating *between* judging and perceiving, and finally

---

5   Kirton, M.J. "Adaptors and Innovators: a description of a measure," *Journal of Applied Psychology* 61, 1976, pp. 622–629.
6   Kirton, M.J. (ed.) *Adaptors and Innovators: styles of creativity and problem solving*, New York: Routledge, 1994.

check their feelings *through* thinking. An additional finding is that culture often determines the extreme side that respondents start from. We're not saying that one culture is more creative than another; only that their starting points for looking at a problem are different.

An inability to combine opposing logics shows an absence of creativity. So, instead of questions from Kirton's original KAI that are based on linear (Likert) scales, our "integrated innovation indicator" asks questions in the following format:

Q1 Which of the following four options best describes how you most frequently behave?

A) I am efficient, thorough, adaptable, methodical, organized, precise, reliable and dependable. (5 score in invention, 0 score in adaptation, 0 score in innovation)
B) I am ingenious, original, independent, unconventional and unpredictable. (0 score in invention, 5 score in adaptation, 0 score in innovation)
C) I am continuously checking in an organized and methodical manner whether my original ideas work in practice. (5 score in invention, 0 score in adaptation, 8 score in innovation)
D) I am methodical and organized first, to set the basis for launching my unconventional ideas. (0 score in invention, 5 score in adaptation, 8 score in innovation)

This can also be shown graphically, as in figure 2.21.

Once we knew that the American professionals scored significantly more B (78%) and D (11%), whilst the Danish professionals scored significantly more A and C (which we expected) we ran development programs to foster a professional style of A (54%) and C (28%), both leading to higher innovation.

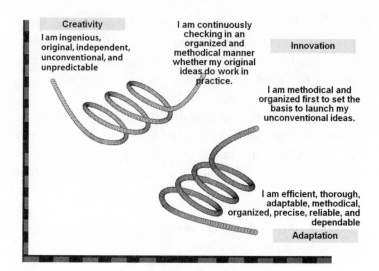

Figure 2.21 Integrated innovation indicator graphic

We designed a training program which stimulated the professionals across the legacy companies to reconcile their (mostly R&D) dilemmas through a C or D mindset. Every six months professionals had to complete the Integrated Kirton Questionnaire (with four options), and this was validated by 360° peer review. This output indicator was taken as one of the main measures of progress.

This case illustrates how the integration process can be guided through the right intervention processes—here the innovative mindset of the organization. From that point we introduced the building of a culture of innovation by integrating the dominant Danish Incubator culture with the US Guided Missile culture through the intermediate Family culture. In the first stage this meant that the Danish and US operations worked on the following dilemmas:

- Leading participating employees vs. Respect for authority.
- Team spirit vs. Individual creativity.

- Effectiveness of teams vs. Creation of cultural knowledge about these teams.
- Lord, servant, or servant leader?
- How do we centralize lessons reaching us from decentralized locations?
- Social learning vs. Technological learning.

Progress on the reconciliations of these dilemmas was monitored with purpose-designed, online "outcome" indicators.

"Outcome" indicators

We define outcome targets as indicators of performance improvement that are relevant for the newly created organization, such as market share and profitability. A very specific way of monitoring the "outcomes" is to rephrase the business challenges as dilemmas and make specific KRIs for the achievement of their reconciliations. The ongoing reconciliations process and monitoring of its progress can be implemented online. This is achieved through our Dilemma Community OnLine (DCOL) and enables participants to share reconciliations and offer inputs and critiques to dilemmas faced by other teams and business units. A hierarchical password system controls which dilemmas can be accessed, e.g., restricted to their own work team, their department, functional area or organization as a whole. Examples are shown in figures 2.22 through to 2.24.

We also provide an online forum and/or instant messaging ("chat version"), allowing different groups to interact and contribute to the reconciliations and have tutorial contact with us, as shown in figure 2.25.

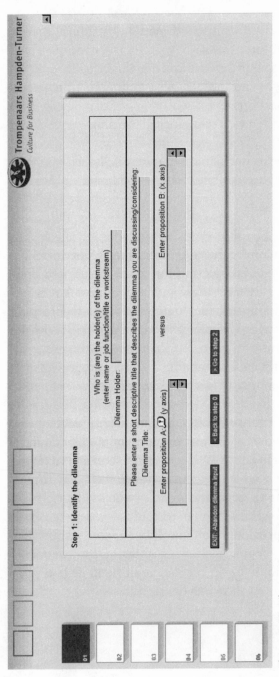

Figure 2.22 Dilemma Community OnLine 1

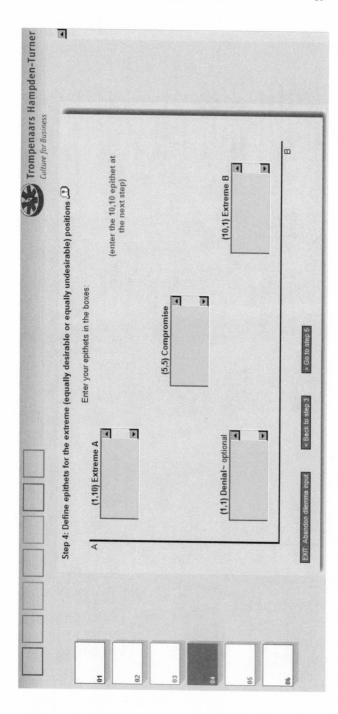

Figure 2.23 Dilemma Community OnLine 2

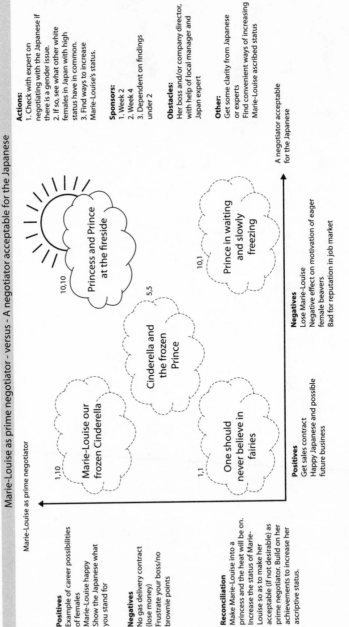

Figure 2.24 Dilemma Community OnLine 3

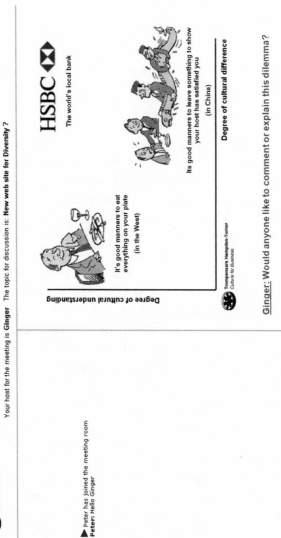

Figure 2.25 Dilemma Community OnLine 4

In the Danish-US pharmaceutical case much attention was given to the reconciliation of the following three dilemmas (from a total of six):

1 Team spirit vs. Individual creativity.
2 Leading participating employees vs. Respect for authority.
3 Lord, servant, or servant leader?

We can interpret the first dilemma concerning individual versus team with insight derived from the concept of *Co-Opetition*: that the membership of teams must be diverse, consisting of people whose values and endowments are opposite, yet these teams must achieve a unity of purpose and shared solutions. Once again, we have two polarized extremes: the *prima donnas* facing up to the cooperative.

The effective leader can mold an effective team out of creative individuals. In turn, the team is made accountable for supporting the creative genius of individuals as they strive to contribute their best to the team.

At NewPharmCo (figure 2.26), there was no problem in finding enough individuals to generate ideas—especially with the Danish onboard. The challenge was the "business system" or community, which had to translate those ideas into the reality of viable products and services. It was not unusual for the American system to impede the realization of good ideas.

The management team of NewPharmCo has made a vital intervention. While ideas originate with individuals, it is insufficient to then simply pass them down to subordinates, who are inhibited in their criticism, for implementation. It required consultants to legitimize skepticism. It was agreed that the originator of an idea must work with critics, implementers and builders of working prototypes to help to debug his/her idea, where necessary.

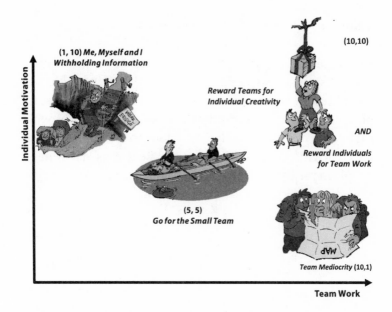

Figure 2.26 NewPharmCo graphic

The top team has seen that it is ineffective to give high status to the idea (rather than to those who implement it). This approach had led to defective ideas, disappointing their backers. Conceptualization and realization are equally important and the two must be reconciled. Ideas must be tested to the point of either destruction or success. This creates the potential for producing a solution that has benefited from diverse viewpoints, novel inputs, and quality that has already cleared the hurdles of skepticism.

The problem with highly diverse, competing individuals is that they may behave like many *prima donnas*, singing their own praises. The problem with unity and team spirit, above all, is that diverse and novel inputs get squeezed out. Reconciliation makes the goal so exciting and the process of creating new shared realities so passionate and enjoyable that diverse members overcome their differences and realize a unity-of-diversities, which makes the solution far more valuable.

In order to stimulate this process of co-opetition a reward system was designed where 50% of variable pay was based on how good individuals were seen to be as team players and 50% was paid to teams on the basis of what they could demonstrate they had done to stimulate individual creativity. The graphic in figure 2.26 was used to remind people in the organization of its importance.

PHASE C: REALIZING AND ROOTING THE BENEFITS

After completion of all the preceding activities, we arrive at the third and last phase. This is the rooting and realization of the previous activities to develop systemic alignment and value awareness. To reiterate, there are three steps in this phase:

8 *Systemic alignment*
9 *Value and cultural awareness programs*
10 *Continuous re-evaluation: monitoring change towards the hyper-culture*

Step 8: Systemic alignment

This part of the process is aimed at keeping everyone aligned. At this stage the leadership team has enough information to develop a detailed implementation program. They have compelling reasons for the integration, they have customized this communication so it aligns with the key drivers of the total population, and they have a clear sense of collective direction, vision and mission; they know the core values, principles and (key) purpose, and they have a set of behaviors that guide, their day-to-day decision making and actions.

The challenge now is to help the CEO and leadership team in making the vision, mission, values and behavior permeate the culture/organization.

There are three major components to the integration process in bringing about a shift in the individual and collective behaviors of the executive population:

- Personal alignment;
- Group alignment and cohesion (values alignment and mission alignment);
- Structural alignment.

The purpose of the personal alignment and group-cohesion programs is to give the integration process a head start by focusing on the alignment of values with the vision and mission of the top team and those who report to the top team (top 100 or so). These executives will be the guardians of the new hyper-culture.

Personal alignment

Having made a start in supporting the leadership team to "walk the talk" with the V2B exercise, we can now align the personal values of the larger executive population with the core values of the new organization. The focus now shifts to personal programs to support the executive population in aligning their personal values with the (newly) defined shared core values.

A personal alignment program (typically a two day workshop) is usually run with intact teams, but the focus is on the development of the individual. A variety of instruments are used.

Alongside the Personal Values Profiler (PVP) we use our Intercultural Competence Profiler (ICP). The ICP enables an organization to assess the current intercultural awareness and abilities of employees as a predictor of effectiveness in multi-cultural or international and/or merger business environments. It can also be used as an indicator of where training may be helpful. The ICP addresses the complete spectrum of cultural behavior from cross-cultural awareness through to the business benefits deriving from effective action in post-merger situations. We have recently used the ICP to enhance the skills of leaders in taking advantage of diversity in a merger or acquisition situation.

The ICP was developed by combining our earlier frameworks based on extensive research and our intellectual property that originally addressed each area separately. Each component has been subjected to rigorous research and testing through many PhD projects plus extensive application in many client situations across the world. Recently we have confirmed the reliability of the combined integrated instrument with a sample base that has included MBA students as well as senior managers and business leaders from our client base. It comprises some 100 questions that are used in different combinations to achieve the total profile. Ratings are not simply added and averaged for the different scales. In many cases the sectors are computed from the RMS quadrature[1] of competing questions to assess their mutual interaction. We developed this ICP because we recognized the limitations of our own earlier cross-cultural instruments that positioned people on bipolar scales of mutually exclusive extremes of seven dimensions.

---

1 For example, a contributing component score might be the square root (Question A score × Question B score).

The ICP instrument

Daily life in the intercultural arena involves judgments, decisions, and actions which, however minor in themselves, in the aggregate affect not only our own lives but those of other individuals and possibly even the future of our society.

Our ICP is an attempt to describe and measure certain modes of thought, sensitivities, intellectual skills, and explanatory capacities which might in some measure contribute to the formation of an intercultural competence.

We distinguish four aspects of intercultural competence:

1 **Recognition:** *How competent is a person in recognizing cultural differences?*
2 **Respect:** *How respectful is a person about those differences?*
3 **Reconciliation:** *How competent is a person in reconciling cultural differences?*
4 **Realization:** *How competent is a person in realizing the necessary actions to implement the reconciliation of cultural differences?*

The graph shown in figure 2.27 defines the various aspects of intercultural competence.

Recognition

Recognizing cultural differences has to do with the individual's ability to understand his or her condition in the community and the world. Skill in this area improves the ability to make effective judgments. It includes the study of nations, cultures, and civilizations, including our own society and the societies of other people, with a focus on

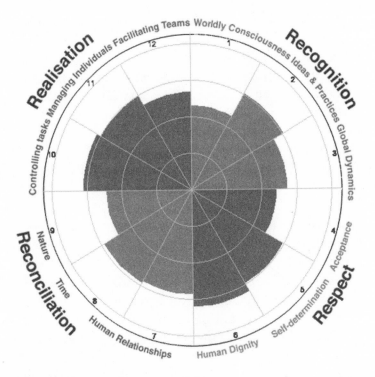

Figure 2.27 Intercultural competence graph

understanding how these are interconnected and how they change, and on the individual's responsibility in this process. It defines some key elements of what we call a global consciousness—to flesh out some of the things we need to know and understand if we are to cope with the challenges of an increasingly interdependent world.

Operationally, we assume that it consists *partly* of the modes of thought, skills, etc. But as conceived here a recognition competence is not a quantum, something you either have or don't have. It is a blend of many things and any given individual may be rich in certain elements and relatively lacking in others. A very crucial part of intercultural awareness as Eileen Sheridan (2005) found in her Delphi-based research is *self-awareness*.

In the competence of recognition, very much according to the description of Robert G. Hanvey (2004), we distinguish three main areas:

Worldly consciousness
The worldly consciousness consists of the following two aspects:

- **Perspective consciousness** is the recognition or awareness on the part of the individual that he or she has a view of the world that is not universally shared, that this view of the world has been and continues to be shaped by influences that often escape conscious detection and that others have views of the world that are profoundly different from one's own. Perspective consciousness is an essential element of self-awareness, assuming the road to discovering oneself is through the contrast with others.

- **"State of the Planet" awareness** is an awareness of prevailing world conditions and development, including emerging conditions and trends, e.g., population growth, migrations, economic conditions, resources and physical environment, political developments, science and technology, law, health, international and intra-national conflicts, etc.

Cross-cultural awareness
This is an awareness of the diversity of ideas and practices to be found in human societies around the world, of how such ideas and practices compare, including some recognition of how the ideas and ways of one's own society might

be viewed from other vantage points. Again, cross-cultural self-awareness is the result of this endeavour to compare oneself against others.

Global dynamics

Part of intercultural competence is to be able to have a prime awareness that ultimately the world is a product of human interactions. According to Hanvey it consists of:

Knowledge of Global Dynamics—Some modest comprehension of key traits and mechanisms of the world system, with an emphasis on theories and concepts that may increase intelligent consciousness of global change.

Awareness of Human Choices—Some awareness of the problems of choice confronting individuals, nations, and the human species as consciousness and knowledge of the global system expands.

The questions we have developed to measure the recognition part of the ICP have many sources such as the ideas developed by Van der Zee and Brinkmann (2002), Lynn Rew, et al. (2003), and in particular Robert G. Hanvey (2004) in *An Attainable Global Perspective*.

Respect

How respectful is a person about those differences? Respect serves as the basis for our attitudinal, cognitive and behavioral orientation towards people who hold a diversity of values. In our professional practice we have focused much of our work on helping people to recognize cultural differences. Entrenchment of stereotypes is a risk of stopping at the level of awareness and recognition. Respect is crucial to competence in dealing with cultural differences.

Webster's Dictionary defines the noun *respect* as "the giving of particular attention, high or special regard, and expressions of deference." As a verb, "to respect" is to consider another worthy of esteem, to refrain from obtruding or interfering, to be concerned, and to show deference. We can create a composite definition of respect that reflects these characteriztics:

> *Respect is a basic moral principle and human right that is accountable to the values of human dignity, worthiness, uniqueness of persons and self-determination. As a guiding principle for actions toward others, respect is conveyed through the unconditional acceptance, recognition and acknowledgment of the intrinsic value of all people.*

Respect is the basis for our attitudinal, cognitive and behavioral orientation. We use the three categories of respect identified by Kelly (1987) as they are helpful for organizing the measurement of respect as an attitude. These categories are:

1 **Respect for human dignity and the uniqueness of a person from another culture.** This means that one would treat other people equally regardless of who they are (dignity and inherent worth). It means that a person is open towards the different working habits of others and tends to question the norms and values of their own culture. Self-assessment is helpful in this case, "How do others see me?" or, "How do others view behavior that I regard as normal?"

2 **Respect for rights to self-determination.** In this second level of respect one considers another person's opinion when planning interactions or elicits suggestions for a plan of action (self-determination). Competence means that one respects the different goals of others; one is at ease with those who hold different views or values. If we

avoid making a judgment on first impressions, we will be more likely to check with others and clarify meaning.

3 **Acceptance of another culture's values.** On the third level of respect we try to measure whether, if you had a choice, you would rather deal or not deal with a person from another culture. People with a highly developed competence tend to enjoy variety and diversity and are open to new ideas. In this case, one is seeking new insights and ways of understanding issues and positively welcomes people who are different

Reconciliation

When an individual recognizes cultural differences and ultimately reconciles them by transforming conflicting values into complementary values[2] they display a competence close to the creativity a person displays in combining values that are, at first sight, contradictory.

As a competent reconciler you have to inspire as well as listen. You have to make decisions yourself but also delegate, and you need to centralize your organization around local responsibilities. As a competent professional, you need to master your materials and at the same time you need to be passionately at one with the mission of the whole organization. You need to apply your analytical skills in placing these contributions in a larger context.

We can identify certain categories of reconciliation and assess an individual's ability with a series of questions in the following areas. Though the questions are asked in a linear fashion, by combining them we see when people have scored high on both by adding to the score on the reconciliation side of this competence. Next to the reconciliation

2 Hampden-Turner, C. & Trompenaars, F. *Building Cross-Cultural Competence*, John Wiley & Sons, 2000.

score, we are also able to see the preferences for the seven dimensions, depending on which of the linear scales one scores highest on.

Standard and adaptation

Do we need to globalize our approach or do we need to localize? Is it more beneficial for our organization to choose mass production or to focus on specialized products? Competent people find the solution in the "transnational organization" where the best local practices are being globalized on a continuous basis. "Mass customization" is the keyword for reconciling standardized production and specialized adaptations.

Individual creativity and team spirit

This dilemma looks for competence in integrating team spirit with individual creativity and a competitive mindset. The competent person knows how to make an excellent team out of creative individuals. The team is stimulated to support brilliant individuals, while these individuals deploy themselves for the greater whole. This has been called co-opetition.

Passion and control

Is a competent person an emotional and passionate person or does the control of emotions make a better person? Here there are two clear types. Passionate people without reason are neurotics, and neutral individuals without emotions are robots. An effective person regularly checks his or her passion with reason, and if we look at more neutral people, we often see individuals who give controlled reason meaning by showing passion once in a while.

Analysis and synthesis

Is the competent person a detached, analytical person who is able to divide the big picture into bite-size pieces, always selecting for shareholder value? Or is it somebody who puts issues in the big picture and gives priority to the rather vague statement "stakeholder value"? At Shell, Van Lennep's "helicopter view" was introduced as a significant characteristic of a modern leader—the ability to ascend and keep the overview, while being able to zoom in on certain aspects of the matter. This is another significant characteristic of the competent reconciler, namely the ability to know when and where to go in deep. Pure analysis leads to paralysis, and the overuse of synthesis leads to an infinite overview and a lack of action.

Doing and being

"Getting things done" is an important characteristic of a manager. However, shouldn't we keep the rather vulgar "doing" in balance with "being," as in our private lives? As a reconciler you have to be yourself as well. From our research it appears that successful reconcilers act the way they really are. They seem to be at one with the business they are undertaking. One of the important causes of stress is that "doing" and "being" are not integrated. Excessive compulsion to perform, when not matching someone's true personality, leads to ineffective behavior.

Reconciling aspects of time: *sequential and parallel*

Notably, effective reconcilers are able to plan in a rigorous sequential way, but at the same time have the ability to stimulate parallel processes. This reconciliation, which we know as "synchronize processes to increase the sequential speed"—or "just in time" management—also seems to be very effective in integrating the long and short term.

Reconciling the inner and the outer worlds: *push and pull*

This final component for today's reconcilers is the ability to connect the voice of the market with the technology the company has developed and vice versa. This is not about technology push or market pull. The competent reconciler knows that the push of technology finally leads to the ultimate niche market, that part without any clients. But if you only choose for the market, the client will be dissatisfied.

Realization

After we have recognized, respected and reconciled cultural differences our task is to develop a process in which the **resolutions are implemented and rooted** in the organization.

This component is well described by John Adair in his action-centerd leadership model.[3] Competent managers and leaders should have full command of three main areas of the action-centerd leadership model (detailed below), and should be able to use each of the elements according to the requirements of the situation.

Being able to be effective in all of these, and keep the right balance, gets results, builds morale, improves quality, develops teams and productivity, and is the mark of a successful manager and leader. The key to nurturing leaders is to make sure your company recognizes excellence at three levels: strategic, operational, and team. "It is a common fallacy that all an organization needs is a good strategic leader at the helm," writes Adair.

Achieving the task

A manager competent in achieving the task is a person who identifies aims and visions for the group connecting a variety of means. He or she identifies resources, people, processes, systems and tools that help implementation and establish

---

3 Interview with John Adair: *Strategic Direction* 2007, Vol 23, Issue: 4, pp. 30–32, Emerald Group Publishing Limited.

responsibilities, objectives, accountabilities and measures. Competence is shown in setting standards, quality, time and reporting parameters and in monitoring and maintaining overall progress toward implementation.

Managing the team or group

The competent implementer for the group establishes, agrees and communicates standards of performance, behavior and shared values. He or she monitors and maintains discipline, ethics, integrity and focus on objectives and resolves group conflict, struggles or disagreements. This competent manager looks for complementarities in the composition of the group and develops the collective capability. He or she motivates the group and provides a collective sense of purpose and identifies, develops and agrees team- and project-leadership roles.

Managing individuals

The manager needs an understanding of the team members as individuals—personality, skills, strengths, needs, aims and fears. He or she gives recognition and praise to individuals—acknowledges effort and good work and identifies, develops and utilizes each individual's capabilities in setting targets and goals. He or she develops individual freedom and authority and encourages personal development.

The ICP results

The ICP is normally completed online, generating personal feedback immediately. On completion, participants can download and save their own personal profile report as a PDF file for archiving and/or printing. Extensive feedback, extended interpretations and theoretical background to the ICP are available in a series of interactive web pages at the web-based ICP support center. Participants can explore their own personal profile through these online tutorials that offer further insights, "coaching" advice and suggestions for development.

To accommodate different client/participant needs we have developed several versions. Thus in the 360° version, a participant's own self-assessment scores can be triangulated with peer feedback. This can even be based on additional input from clients, customers and/or suppliers. The "organization version" is oriented to an analysis of the "competence" of the business unit and/or wider organization rather than the individual. In the "diversity" version, the focus is on diversity and ethnicity rather than country derived cultures.

Data we have collected has already demonstrated that ICP profiling provides an objective measure for both the individual and the organization. Significantly it reveals key support needs: does the client need cross-cultural awareness training or leadership development, for example? And, of course, "before" and "after" measurements provide evidence of the impact of any intervention that can be correlated with improved business performance.

The PVP instrument

Using the Personal Value Profiler alongside OVP demonstrates the contrasts between personal and organizational values. This stage focuses on helping the individual participants to reconcile the values in a DRP enriching process. Personalized coaching will help the participants to extend their mindset by defining a personal roadmap to integrate personal with corporate values. Coaching sessions will also inform participants of how to further develop their competencies to reconcile value differences across organizational, national and functional cultures.

Such programs can be designed for the top three layers of the organization.

Group alignment and cohesion (values alignment and mission alignment)
This provides the intact team with feedback on the degree of alignment between the current and desired culture of their business or functional unit. We use the OVP output as the base starting point. The performance gaps are used to identify the underlying dilemmas between current and ideal and the DRP session is used to close these gaps through reconciliation. This step ends with a set of action points and a link to the core values of the organization and an exercise in translating the values to the group (V2B).

Structural alignment
The aim of the structural alignment program is to reconfigure the systems and processes of the organization so that they align with the vision, mission, values, purpose and behaviors of the organization.

It redefines systems and processes such as:

- Executive selection and orientation;
- Executive performance evaluation and promotion criteria;
- Appraisal systems;
- Leadership development programs;
- Management training programs and value and cultural awareness programs.

Step 9: Value and cultural awareness programs

The value and cultural awareness programs extend throughout the organization to make employees aware of the major differences in corporate and national cultures and how to take advantage of those differences within the shared envisioned future, core values and purpose of the organization. These are conducted as one- or two-day workshops and begin with an introduction from at least two senior leaders who explain the compelling reasons for the integration, then outline the vision, mission, values and behaviors and the structural alignment program, including specific objectives and KRIs. Simulations and case studies illustrate how important values are in attaining changes in the business approach such as how to work with clients, behavior towards colleagues and managing change. The result is greater awareness of the importance of value differences and value similarities in the process of attaining business success.

This program uses a "blended learning" approach and employs tools like our web based Culture Compass OnLine (CCOL), which includes the assessment of individual value orientations through our Intercultural Assessment Profiler (IAP). The results of the outputs/action points of the major dilemmas are reviewed by the senior leaders of the new organization.

In situations where international differences play a key role and understanding of those differences makes a crucial contribution to business effectiveness, setting up an Intercultural Competence Center or team is highly recommended. This can support the organization's strategy through relevant intercultural training, consulting and coaching initiatives; it can help to define the intercultural competencies that managers and staff members need to manage the increased complexity of their international environment; and it could, if applicable, include country specific workshops to increase awareness and competence in dealing with specific national cultures.

Sustaining the initiatives

Theater, story-telling and art workshops are also highly effective in creating values awareness. After increasing awareness, specific projects can be defined in which the participants can contribute to the major dilemmas that the senior leadership has identified. These projects might include topics such as brand image, corruption, promotion criteria for managers, quality improvement, diversity and so forth.

Finally, it is important to recognize that in some situations it is more effective to start with the values and cultural awareness programs before getting to the personal and group alignment programs after appropriate adjustments are made.

Progress is monitored using a set of integrated scorecards which help guide and assess the major value tensions between personal, cultural and core values.

Step 10: Continuous re-evaluation: monitoring change towards the hyper-culture

The progress and speed of the integration process depends largely on the actual situation. Every merger requires specific plans, interventions and monitoring systems. Once you move into full-fledged preparation and beyond, there are some checklists available to monitor the progress of implementation at individual, company and unit level. These checklists can be integrated into ongoing assessments such as employee surveys, engagement surveys, etc.

These checklists, combined with the online check on progress on the reconciliation of main dilemmas, OVP and the instruments measuring the KRIs in HR systems mean that we can keep a finger on the pulse of an organization, and targeted interventions can be made immediately if a problem or need is identified.

PART III

The business of relationships and dilemmas

In this part of the book we analyze trust, basic assumptions, and the human relationships that build upon these. Beyond that, we will investigate the systemic dualities or dilemmas that form the basis of business discontent with integration successes. This offers the reader deeper insights into the sources of dilemmas and value differences to give further assistance in the application of the ten step framework.

In most mergers and acquisitions, two groups with years of consistent behaviors and assumptions about how life needs to be approached come together. Many assumptions are challenged. What was taken for granted can't be taken for granted any longer. This is a genuine culture shock, and people start doubting the consistency of giving and getting feedback, from clients, colleagues, and management. The issue of trust has been aptly described as one of the most fundamental values in business and personal relationships. Many books and research projects have attempted to define and qualify the value of trust; from Francis Fukuyama's groundbreaking work *Trust: The Social Value and the Creation of Prosperity* (1996, the Free Press) to the more recent attempts to accelerate trust building by Stephen Covey and Rebecca Merrill in *The Speed of Trust: The One Thing That Changes Everything* (2008, the Free Press).

Most books about trust focus on the need for consistency, which is often damaged or at least challenged in the merger process. The repair process is a long-term integration challenge.

Trust

Trust, honesty and transparency create substantial business value. Businesses create wealth and sustainability based upon the strength and agility (not simply power) of trust-worthy relationships, and consistency goes a long way to "proving" the trust of a relationship. For consistency to be adequately measured, we need to align our vision, mission, purpose and strategy. If there is no alignment, or at the very least the hope of a positive outcome in a business transaction, there is no commitment to trust. We want to believe, yet not be naive about, an agreement between two well-intentioned and hopeful merchants. Time and technology have made us change the way we trust. Once we could say "my word is my bond," walk away and expect to conclude the business deal another day. That time is past, although the principle still stands. The business culture of today still acknowledges the sentiment carried in the age-old phrase, which adorns the London Stock Exchange, but we are now interacting on a higher scale of complexity and have higher rates of interaction through various technology-enhanced communication systems. Computers have made it possible to transact many more products and services across a vast and complex network of relationships.

Businesses build empires on the basis of these tangled relationships, and they appear to be able to measure the risk of losing trust in all of these. Rarely, do we hear about trust being abused in the way that has recently rocked the banking industry (Lehman Brothers collapse, Madoff, bank bail-outs, etc.) and before that in the accounting world (Enron, Arthur Andersen, Worldcom, etc.). These fallouts appear to indicate that we have such deeply held beliefs associated with trust that some financial entities actually thought that the complexity of the relationships that they managed created a trust that would be too large to fail. We also learned that too much consistency of profits and margins comes at a great cost, no matter how much we want to put our trust in that consistency of payouts.

Of course, it is important to address the underlying motivations for creating and pursuing "trustworthy" professional business as well as personal relationships as we do not wish to become a victim of any kind of abuse. Some motivators (excessive short-term bonus schemes, for example) can create trust destroying cultures. Although these cultures could be highly beneficial for a happy few in the short term, the individual benefit is not measured against the societal benefit that the institution/organization is meant to serve. As we will explain, gaining trust requires the reconciliation of individual and communitarian motivators. We consider three levels of trust that will help us to dissect the different relationships that impact on roles and motivations in business (figure 3.1).[1]

Three levels of trust

1 **Structural trust** can be identified as the trust embedded in the organizational structure of the business. In this context, we talk about the governance of the business, its plans to globalize or localize, and the challenges of centralization versus decentralization. Is the business structurally sound enough to withstand the trials and tribulations of the industry it operates in? With this comes a sense of history (how long has it been successful), questions around rigidity as well as flexibility towards specific needs, questions about scale and scope, and operating structures that could match specific customer needs. In short, structural trust provides an expression of the structural alignment of the organization with its strategic plans.

2 **Professional trust** goes to the expertise of the organization and its employees (experts) that is required to address the needs of the customer. Can that level of

---

1 Adapted from Saj-Nicole Joni, *The Third Opinion*, Portfolio, 2004.

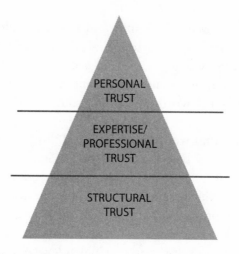

Figure 3.1 The trust pyramid

expertise be trusted to achieve the strategic goals of the organization? Individually, can I trust the expertise of my colleagues to create an environment that sustains my motivation and warrants my contribution?

3 **Personal trust** is a deeply felt belief and assumption that the parties "belong" together and share a bond that cannot be broken. Personal trust in relationships grows by sharing common interests, and traits, unrelated to or separate from professional interests. Seeking to find something unique in ourselves, we are eager to share it with someone who appears to recognize and deeply respect that uniqueness. In the personal relationship, we share what is common and what is unique and build trustworthiness out of the interaction of the two. Great leaders know that strengthening business relationships doesn't simply depend on formal reviews. Most leaders seek informal ways to convey important issues to employees as well. Jack Welch once stated that he reviewed the business challenges with his direct subordinates at least six times a year. Two of those six times

were informal. These informal reviews could be done while attending a barbecue, at a casual family dinner, or during a day off playing golf. The reconciliation between informal and formal interaction increases the personal trustworthiness of the relationship.

It is unlikely that we would achieve all three levels of trust with any and all business partners. During a merger process it is important to increase the trust and communication both between the merging entities and between the different levels of the companies. Increasing the number and intensity of interactions between specific groups of both companies accelerates the development of a higher level of understanding and respect for professional expertise.

It is important to thoroughly assess the individuals charged with important parts of the integration process. In this assessment, we generally identify and clarify underlying assumptions about norms, values, and the artifacts of business relationships. Recognizing and respecting these assumptions emboldens the trust factor. For years, the Trompenaars Hampden-Turner group has studied basic assumptions and motivators from a cross-cultural perspective to describe global corporate cultures and the challenges businesses face when they merge and integrate across boundaries. The following section elaborates on the importance of the systematic assessment of these assumptions in dimensions of human relationships.

Basic assumptions and dimensions of human relationships

We all, in our own way—and influenced as we are by our upbringing, our families, our education, our culture, and the organizations we associate with (work and leisure)— develop motivators for trust. We are often unaware of the way we seek trust and very few of us actively examine how we come to build trust. More often than not we have certain assumptions about trust, and sometimes even claim to know what it should look and feel like. Perhaps it is useful to establish that trust needs to be an input as well as an output of any new or old relationship.

Identifying what the motivators of trust are and finding the roots and building blocks for trust in our lives begins and ends with identifying what and how we communicate. We constantly communicate values. These values are based on core beliefs about ourselves, feedback from family and friends, and the trust we communicate to others. The way we are perceived through non-verbal and verbal communication influences the way we build the trust pyramid shown in figure 3.1. Understanding which values we are communicating and radiating through our business presence becomes increasingly important as we move up the corporate ladder.

Basic assumptions are the basis upon which values, beliefs, behaviors and actions are constructed. The most basic motivator is our shared need to survive our environment (figure 3.2).

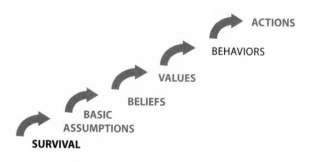

Figure 3.2 Cumulative basic assumptions

Through our 20-year research on cultural differences in business, we have come to identify dimensions of basic assumptions that indicate value differences and seemingly opposing motivators for trust. This organization of meaning in human relationships with other humans, time and nature has been well documented and referenced, and we provide only a brief overview here. It provides a strong measure for identifying what value orientations we use to initiate relationships. The subsequent process we developed with our clientele has delivered invaluable insights into how we develop trust as an output and an input to a relationship management process, which has a massive impact on the successful integration of people through restructuring, reorganization, merging or acquiring.

But let's look at the dimensions of human relationships first and identify the underlying basic assumptions and motivators for initial trust.

Seven dimensions of human relationships in building trust

The dimensions indicated in figure 3.3 display various ways of assessing relationships. Depending on our preference for either side of these dimensions, we would initiate relationships and expect trust to be built in particular ways. Our initial preference has a direct effect on the type of relationships we prefer to forge. We can measure groups of participants and point out where the strengths and weaknesses can be found in a team. We have also managed to identify corporate cultures based on these dimensions and can match these against another corporate culture in the case of a merger or acquisition.

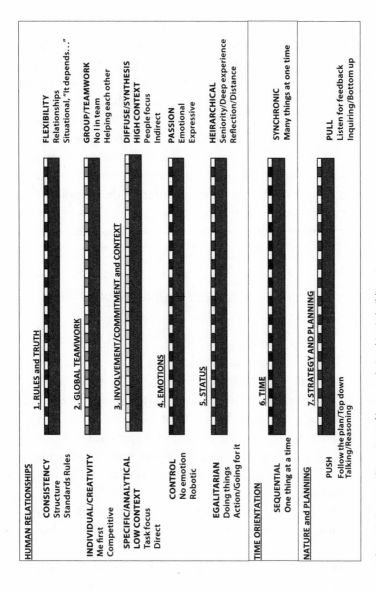

Figure 3.3 Seven dimensions of human relationships in building trust

As can be seen in figure 3.3, the measurement of the basis of these dimensions is still fairly linear. Whether the score is higher on consistency or on flexibility, it is still an either/or situation. This is because in our work we have found that all human beings and all teams have and need both orientations for full meaning. What we try to measure is the preference for starting the reconciliation process on either end of the dimension, which creates trust. All individuals and all cultures need rules and exceptions. In some cultures people start with rules in order to then challenge those with exceptions. In other cultures there is a preference for starting with exceptions from which general rules are derived.

The process of trust building and the integration of the dimensions of culture

The real value of our earlier research on the dimensions of culture lies in each one of the extremes of the dimensions themselves and the combination of these to illuminate a systemic approach to value creation that is sustainable and motivating, and therefore begets trust.

To overcome the linear and strictly analytical process of assessment and find a more engaging way of assessing the value of relationships, we decided to create a dual axis graph, shown in figure 3.4, upon which we could map seemingly opposing value orientations from both sides of the dimensions, and start to uncover the process of building trust.

From this picture it is obvious that the two seemingly opposing sides of the dimension will have to communicate in order to resolve their differences. As both sides are essentially positive in their connotations, we identify such challenges as dilemmas.

CONSISTENCY
Structure,
Standards, Rules

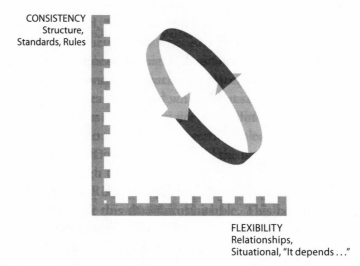

FLEXIBILITY
Relationships,
Situational, "It depends..."

Figure 3.4 Dual axis trust map

As leaders, teams and larger cultures, we share the same dilemmas, but we have different approaches to integrating the opposing dualities. A leader needs to set rules and appreciate exceptions, be persistent and flexible, be a team player and excel as an individual, show passion and be reasonable at the same time. All leaders need to be able to understand the big picture and the minute detail, be a servant and lead the gang, push the organization's products and listen to the latest needs of the clients. These dilemmas can be reconciled within cultures and between individuals where there is a consistent order. It is in this consistency that trust is built. It leads to mutual expectations, a crucial aspect of culture, that is reinforced regularly, leading to an ever-increasing system of trust.

The difference between cultures doesn't lie in the different type of dilemmas being faced but in the order in which they are taken and reconciled. We realize that we have different categories of trust, different entry points for engaging in a potentially trustworthy relationship, and we realize that we will have to find a way to reconcile the differences between our points of view. The ensuing dilemmas can be organized and categorized. Understanding a successful merger as the reconciliation of a good number of dilemmas goes a long way to understanding a successful integration process.

"Ten Golden Dilemmas"

We have collected some 9,000 dilemmas during our research and consulting, including around 1,500 relating to mergers and acquisitions. These dilemmas can be categorized/clustered as ten frequently recurring dilemmas. We have validated the derivation of these ten frequently recurring dilemmas both inductively by factor analysis of interview and open question data and deductively by testing propositions. As explained in Part II, we describe these as the "Ten Golden Dilemmas." Every partner organization seems to have different priorities when focusing on these golden dilemmas that need to be reconciled in order to achieve future success and sustainability for the organization.

These generic golden dilemmas manifest themselves in specific ways in the particular circumstances of each merger. The ten golden dilemmas are formed on the basis of the conflicting demands of and relationship between five stakeholders. It is simply not good enough to focus on just one of the points of excellence represented by the stakeholders or on all of them without assessing what happens to the relationships between these. For example, we are generally ill advised to focus exclusively on shareholder value to the detriment of employees or our contribution to society. Banks, insurance companies, and pharmaceutical companies, to name a few that have all been in the news recently, face tough dilemmas in this regard.

Essentially these dilemmas can only be reconciled once we start to measure the success of a decision to optimize one point of excellence (shareholder value for example) in the context of another point of excellence (e.g., contributions to society). In order to remain or become sustainable, all organizations have to pursue these five points of excellence at the same time. A solution that focuses exclusively on one side of one of these dilemmas will not take into account the strength of the combination and the potential to increase learning and the ultimate production of trustworthy outcomes. Organizations and their leaders need to develop an ability to create value from elements that are not easily combined (a dilemma) and the integration must be both tailored to customers' needs and profitable (figure 3.5).

Efficient business processes, best captured in the principles of scientific management, must drive all organizations. Yet at the same time, we must take care of our people. Hence the human relations movement (employee develop-

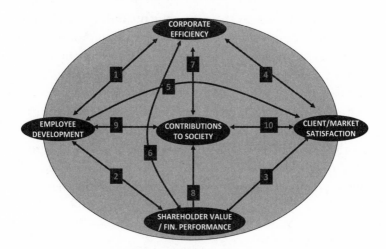

Figure 3.5 Dilemmas of the Sustainable Organization

ment) really only started to take shape after we realized the abuse that was going on in factories. We needed a systematic way to address the sole focus on efficiency of business processes. The efficiency processes were efficient only at the cost of human development. Once we started to invest in human relations development and improved production environments for laborers, we found that efficiency increased as well.[2]

Eventually, it became important to understand our markets better and align our value chains with the needs of the customers. The client orientation of the mid-seventies overthrew the reign of the human relations era. But as with the previous monolithic focus it led to a disproportionate exaggeration. It was all done at the cost of the shareholder . . .

Our next challenge was to become financially sound, perform well, and repay those who put their money at risk with us. Shareholder value and financial performance became the name of the game, but of course, we still needed to be efficient and effective with our business processes and at the same time invest in our people. Shareholders demanded unrealistic returns on their investments and threatened to pull their money out of companies if they did not perform as well as they had hoped they would. Although it may have seemed necessary to tighten up the financial management and performance of organizations it also led to massive fluctuations in available capital for some companies and thus a shift in focus from one side of a dilemma to the other side. Yet the requirements of efficient and effective business processes (scientific management), the human relations focus, client orientation and the shareholder demands had not

---

2   Elton Mayo, *Hawthorne and the Western Electric Company, The Social Problems of an Industrial Civilization*, Routledge, 1949.

ebbed away either, hence we had a variety of dilemmas in front of us.

The last focal point added to the mix for many organizations was to provide "tangible contributions to society." Earlier entitled "corporate social responsibility," the focus has been on gift giving, green production methods, zero emission standards, and many community based initiatives. The crux here is that all these investments have to generate returns of some kind.

The power of looking at this "organization of dilemmas or dilemmas of the organization" is that each individual element can be measured in its singularity, but we get a greater return when looking at them together. Organizational leaders are always focusing on at least two elements that need to be reconciled. Take a look back at the merger goals—these spring from the organizational dilemmas described here. Figure 3.6 shows a generic list of the ten, high-level global dilemmas that organizations are facing across the world.

Simply assessing these dilemmas does not in itself create value, hence the need to work on resolving them. Over the years we have further perfected this dilemma reconciliation process and it has become the principal way for us to explain, measure and process integration to create trust and shared wealth. In this systematic approach:

- Competition and collaboration creates co-opetition;
- Mass market and high volume entwined with customization creates mass-customized value;
- Specific technical expertise matched with diffuse attention to personal requirements and needs creates moments of truth and shared wealth.

Let's explore the point of resolving dilemmas in the next section.

10 Golden Dilemmas

Golden Dilemma	ON THE ONE HAND...	ON THE OTHER HAND...
1	(**Employees**) We need to develop our people for their future roles.	(**Business Processes**) We need to become more cost conscious and results orientated.
2	(**Shareholder**) We need to cut costs wherever we can for the sake of our shareholder's return.	(**Business Processes**) We need to invest for long term sustainability.
3	(**Business Processes**) We need to supply standard products/services as defined from HQ.	(**Clients**) We need to supply products/services that respond to local tastes and needs.
4	(**Busines Processes**) We need to focus on cash flow and working capital.	(**Society**) We need to serve the wider community in a sustainable and responsible way.
5	(**Employees**) We need to motivate and reward our people.	(**Shareholder**) We need to satisfy our shareholder(s).
6	(**Employees**) We need to educate clients/customers with new solutions we can offer.	(**Clients**) We need to keep the customer in focus ahead of our own personal preference.
7	(**Employees**) We need to retain equal opportunities for all exisiting staff.	(**Society**) We need to apply some positive discrimination to increase diversity.
8	(**Employees**) We need to satisfy our client/customer needs.	(**Shareholder**) We need to generate both revenue and capital growth for our shareholders.
9	(**Shareholder**) We need to maximize shareholder return from our existing business.	(**Society**) We need to adapt to the future as society evolves.
10	(**Society**) We need to supply products and services that enhance our reputation in the wider community.	(**Clients**) We need to supply products which our clients and customers are asking for.

Figure 3.6 Top ten global dilemmas

Trust: the point of resolving dilemmas

There are always at least two seemingly opposing approaches to achieving resolution. This conclusion is based on our ongoing studies of global business decision-making processes. Although there are very similar business challenges across the world, we have found that different cultures often go about resolving their problems/challenges in completely different ways. The way Americans approach challenge and crisis is almost opposite to the way their Japanese colleagues would address a crisis situation. Neither is better than the other; they are simply approaching the problem from different ends of the spectrum. The point is that we have to learn from our differences and improve our global capabilities.

By analyzing thousands of business dilemmas from companies around the globe, we have found that there is a way to identify, frame, process, and resolve dilemmas and that this process creates involvement, commitment, dedication, and support for the resolutions that the process creates. This becomes even more apparent when two different organizations come together with a wish to integrate. It is commonplace to see a very client-centric organization taken over by a shareholder-centric organization facing the problem of which paradigm should have dominance. Once a problem is framed as a dilemma and mapped appropriately on our dilemma grids, all participants to the resolution can identify themselves on the dilemma map and are committed to finding an integrated solution. The dilemma map explains differences of opinion and identifies challenges that were previously "invisible." It also provides a direction and a clear visionary description of what a resolution might look like, before we begin to identify the path of integration and resolution.

The illustration in figure 3.7 indicates the current and ideal scores of a group of senior executives on a high level dilemma that their teams had to address in a merger process. There had been a lot of discussion, and frustrations were running high on the lack of progress that was being made on the issue, long before we were asked to facilitate a meeting. We simply asked participants a few questions online, verified that we had the correct framing of the dilemma, and subsequently scored each participant on our dilemma grid. The 15 pairs of dots on the grid and the discrepancy between the scores indicated the wide range of disagreement on the issue between the members of this new executive team. But we were also able to emphasize that they all saw it as a dilemma that needed reconciliation. Seeing their colleagues' interest and willingness to move towards the 10,10 area encouraged them to ask more open questions, identified different approaches to reaching agreement and created a renewed sense of common purpose for the team. The problems were resolved relatively quickly after we performed our conflict resolution interaction and took the team through the steps to reconcile the dilemma. We also brought in the "outliers,"

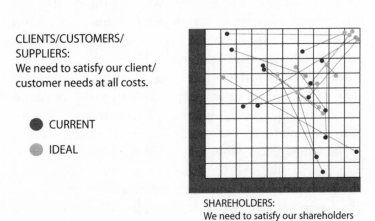

CLIENTS/CUSTOMERS/
SUPPLIERS:
We need to satisfy our client/
customer needs at all costs.

● CURRENT

● IDEAL

SHAREHOLDERS:
We need to satisfy our shareholders

Figure 3.7 Current and ideal perceptions of the dilemma

team members who held potentially contentious viewpoints that could be used to improve the resolution and could therefore no longer be simply ignored.

These maps became dilemma maps or, as some of our workshop participants called them, trust maps. In our workshops, such maps become much more elaborate and constitute a communication tool to reconcile extremely complex issues and contentious points of view between the parties.

The most important challenges in a business merger come to us in the form of dilemmas, but we are trained and accustomed to seeing most problems as requiring a linear solution; we have difficulty framing our issues as dilemmas. The dilemma approach is not stimulated during most of the business management studies that we regularly survey or even participate in. Most are still focused on trying to provide the one "best" way of resolving the issues that are brought forward in elaborate case studies.

Dilemmas offer a method of researching and recognizing our own value orientations and communicating with others about these. The potential confrontation with someone who believes something entirely different yet is willing to find a resolution that combines the strength of both convictions is thrilling and exactly what wealth creation and knowledge sharing is all about. As we have already found in science, interdisciplinary studies are more likely to be truly innovative. People who are able to understand, process, and reconcile dilemmas are inherently more innovative than others. They appear to learn faster than others, and are generally seen as better leaders and managers by others. Our most recent research also shows that those who are skilled in dilemma reconciliation are more likely to be promoted and are better bottom line and profit center leaders as well.[3]

3   Trompenaars, F. *Riding the Whirlwind*, Infinite Ideas, Oxford, 2008; and Hampden-Turner, C. *The Singapore Experiment*, InterCultural Management Publishers, Amsterdam, 2009.

Hence we can conclude that framing dilemmas and reconciling them helps us to identify those crucial value confrontations that are worth pursuing for organizations, teams and individuals as these help us focus on building profitable and sustainable corporations.

In defining human capital and talent management, we require a systematic process and a measure that we can hold up for our employees (human resources). Human resources should be able to leverage capital resources with a multiplier that indicates how our collective intelligence improves the wealth creating moments that our organization supports. Looking at the organization from the perspective of the dilemmas that its employees/leaders have to resolve, and the dilemma reconciliation process that creates the dilemma and trust maps, provides such a multiplier. As the process is entirely inclusive, it also forges many innovative, trusting relationships.

Sustainability, reconciled dilemmas and integration leadership

In order to fully engage human capital in our organizations and create trust and thus wealth, business relationships need to be reframed and restated. Of course, this is especially true for merging and acquiring organizations that are engaging in the complex process of integrating people's talents, skills and, more importantly, motivations.

If our people are our best assets, we should provide human capital tools to address the motivational challenges of building trustworthy human relationships. Trustworthy relationships are the basis for wealth creation. We identify organizational dilemmas, strategic tensions and real integration issues and test the strength of our relationships on these. Embracing the diversity embedded in the organizational relationships ensures a more innovative and inclusive approach to resolving real business challenges.

Instead of attributing power to specific roles, we can begin to attribute specific power and weight to relationships in organizations. Relationships of a strategic, structural, expert, team and individual nature are the engine of an organization's growth and of course the key to creating trust in and between organizations. If these relationships are mapped, then provided with a common soul (values) and a clear vision, we simply have to frame these and have our relevant teams work on the key dilemmas of integrating organizations.

The individual alone cannot create value through his or her actions. The relationship space around that person needs to be filled with other, preferably diverse, people so that the foundation for value creation, *diversity*, is available. The relationship space between people in the organization both creates and supports the value of more than the sum of the people combined. If we apply a multiplier to each relationship that is slightly larger than two, we will be able to measure the effect of multiple relationships much more accurately than by simply attributing so much relational power to the CEO. The value lies in the strength of the relationships between employees at and between all levels.

The strength of the relationships in organizations can be tested by confronting them with structural, strategic, and team dilemmas. The relationships have to be extended to achieve decisions, while involving other relationships depending on the scale of the dilemma. We are frequently faced with organizational dilemmas that the participants are not equipped to handle. In these cases they need to be able to call on the skills of other teams and individuals.

It is important to realize that dilemma reconciliation is a consistent, repeatable, and reliable process that can be taught throughout organization(s). The process also includes assessment tools and automated ways of identifying dilemmas within organizations to avoid expensive large-scale interview arrangements.

When cultural and strategic dilemmas are resolved, they don't simply disappear. New dilemmas occur and we need to apply the process of dilemma reconciliation again and again. Crises are anticipated and dealt with on a continuous basis in organizations. What is different after the first time is that every crisis is framed in the same dilemma format so that everybody can get on the dilemma map quickly, identify where everybody locates themselves, and the team is focused on the resolution path faster. A common understanding of the challenges is mapped out, and the strategic direction can be decided immediately after assessing the pros and cons of each strategic step.

Reconciliations generally remain sustainable, until the environment changes. This usually forces a new and different dilemma rather than another solution from the same dilemma. Nevertheless, the dilemma management process remains the same—reliable, repeatable and consistent— wherever it is applied in the organization.

The dilemma reconciliation process

After years of perfecting and testing our approach with our international client base, we have come to a process description that illuminates four specific process steps. These steps are not just "something to do" at a certain interval. Each step is representative of a learning journey in itself and the four steps can therefore be independently assessed and further developed. Each step illuminates a different part of a mindset change model. We focus here primarily on the practical side of the process to help give more detail than the overview in Part II. This helps us to define and frame a dilemma and subsequently reconcile the challenges and benefits from the integration process.

But first let's look at the practical application of the four steps in our framework that can integrate important dilemmas and create valuable connections between contrasting values.

Step 1: Recognize the dilemma

The first task is to help all players recognize the existence of business differences, their importance and how they impact on business perceptions and results. Culture, like an onion, consists of layers that can be peeled off.

We can distinguish three layers. First, the *outer* layer is what people primarily associate with culture: the visual reality of behavior, clothes, food, language, the organizational chart, the handbook for HR policies, etc. This is the level of explicit culture we referred to earlier.

Second, the *middle* layer refers to the norms and values that an organization holds: what is considered right and wrong (norms) or good and bad (values).

Third, there is the deepest *inner* layer: the level of unquestioned, implicit culture. It is the result of human beings organizing to reconcile frequently occurring dilemmas. It consists of basic assumptions, the routines and methods developed to deal with the regular problems that one faces. These methods of problem solving have become so basic that, like breathing, we no longer think about how we do it.

For an outsider these basic assumptions are very difficult to recognize. Understanding the core of the culture onion is the key to successfully working with other cultures and to successful alliances and cross border collaboration.

Thus, while we instantly recognize the explicit cultural differences, we may not recognize the implicit cultural differences. This explains the common lack of cultural due diligence in pre- and post-merger/acquisition management.

A German electronics company had great audio technology but lacked marketing skills. They decided to buy a US-based client-centric organization to compensate for that weakness. In a team meeting to discuss the marketing of their latest MP3-player, participants from the different organizations didn't realize that some consider an MP3-player to be a device that enables you to listen "to your favorite music without being disturbed" while others consider it to be a device that enables you to listen "to your favorite music without disturbing others!" Such hidden differences require structured processes and an associated competence mindset to reveal underlying problems.

Partners in pre- and post-merger discussions might assume they have common points of view, hold similar value orientations and give similar meaning to the things they are debating, without realizing that they are all talking from different perspectives. When two values are in conflict, it is quite natural to establish the pros and cons of both sides as is illustrated in figure 3.8.

Step 2: Respect the dilemma
Different cultural orientations and views of the world are not right or wrong—they are just different. It is all too easy

Centralization   Decentralizaton

Figure 3.8 Pros and cons

to be judgmental and to distrust those who give different meanings to their world than you do. Thus the next step is to respect these differences and accept the right of others to interpret the world in the way they do.

Because of the different views of the world and different meaning given to apparently similar constructs, we find that these differences manifest themselves as dilemmas. We have two seemingly opposing views, which many people assume have to be represented on a linear, bipolar scale. You can have either one or the other, or more of one and less of the other.

But this thinking is fundamentally flawed and derives from a Cartesian approach which has gained prominence in our Western way of thinking. We need to think differently and open our minds to the possibility of co-existence. By changing the single bipolar line into two axes, we create a "culture space" where we can engage in dialogue and explore new solutions in this new paradigm as is seen in figure 3.9.

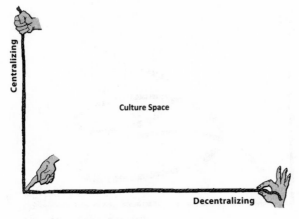

Figure 3.9 Framing tensions as dilemmas

Step 3: Reconcile the dilemma

Our data provides growing evidence that wealth is created in alliances (including mergers and acquisitions) by reconciling values. This is a new contribution to the debate on alliances and mergers in business.

Cultural due diligence is the means to bring about reconciliation of these seemingly opposing views. Our model helps to identify and define behaviors that really make mergers effective. This new approach will inform managers in guiding the social side of alliances of any kind. It has a logic that integrates differences. It is a series of behaviors that enable effective interaction with those of contrasting value systems. It reveals a propensity to share understanding of the position of others in the expectation of reciprocity and requires a new way of thinking that is initially difficult for many Westerners.

We look for ways to realize both values at the same time by asking how we can get more of value A through value B and vice versa. In the example shown in figure 3.10, we would

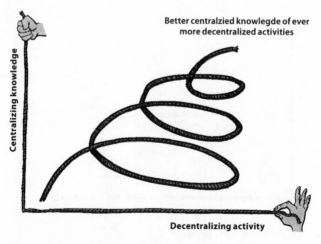

Figure 3.10 The dilemma between centralization and decentralization

be decentralizing activities, while at the same time centralizing knowledge *about* the activities. We are seeking to connect the strength of one extreme with the strength of the other and get not only the best of both, but enrichment through synergy.

Step 4: Realizing and rooting

We now come to the rooting and realization of the previous activities within and across the organization. Here we look at the systemic points where we can make the reconciliation happen and, sometimes even more importantly, sustain it. Do we go for integration in HR processes, or rather go for a new branding strategy? Is it best sustained by a leadership style intervention or by the introduction of an IT and knowledge management solution?

Global dilemmas and integration leadership

Leaders of dilemma reconciliation need to be trained to lead the executive team through the integration process. We have found that their progress can be measured and the process taught. As we researched what good reconcilers actually do, we found that many of them were intuitive integrators. Most of them did not realize how good they were at this, or indeed that they were doing anything at all in terms of specific process steps. It was just the way they went about their job. Some were more reflective in their learning style and had some hint of what process they actually followed in getting their teams to address challenges. But the majority appeared fairly instinctive about it and had great difficultly in making their competence explicit.

Although their subconscious competence is very useful to them, it does not necessarily create the greatest benefit to their organizations, as their skill remains unidentified. Upon testing more than 10,000 leaders and researching the traits and habits of most of them, we discovered the elements that make for these great, instinctive dilemma leaders. We framed their behavior in the same four separate categories of development outlined in the dilemma reconciliation process, and specifically outlined each one of the four categorical steps with three specific elements/competencies that we found in practical research and literature studies to be of vital importance for leaders of global organizations.

Figure 3.11 is effectively a re-statement of our ICP model described in Part II but from the perspective of the competencies required for an effective leader to match our global leadership model.

Using this assessment tool, we can identify the great integrating leaders in organizations and highlight what they are doing. We have found that reconciling leaders are those that create value by constantly integrating differences within their organization as well as between their organization and other organizations, including customers and suppliers. Those that understand their own abilities and respect those of others, and subsequently integrate the differences, generally know how to realize the benefits of dilemmas at the strategic, organizational, team, and individual levels. But we also found that great leaders have the competence to distinguish a dilemma from a problem and make the right choices between them. We have not just been able to successfully assess these leaders, but have also been able to help them by making their implicit competence explicit and therefore trainable and leverage-able throughout the organization. To have a consistent, reliable and repeatable process to integrate value-based elements in an organization is tremendously powerful, particularly because this supports and encourages diversity and innovation.

We have further correlated our findings and scores with many organizations' own measures of successful leadership

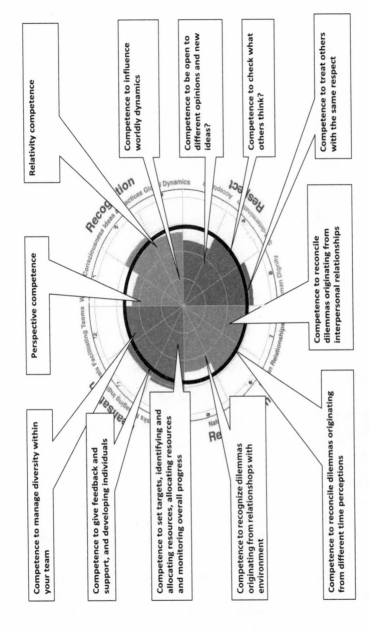

Relativity competence

Competence to influence worldly dynamics

Competence to be open to different opinions and new ideas?

Competence to check what others think?

Competence to treat others with the same respect

Perspective competence

Competence to reconcile dilemmas originating from interpersonal relationships

Competence to manage diversity within your team

Competence to give feedback and support, and developing individuals

Competence to set targets, identifying and allocating resources, allocating resources and monitoring overall progress

Competence to recognize dilemmas originating from relationshops with environment

Competence to reconcile dilemmas originating from different time perceptions

Figure 3.11 Components of intercultural competence

and found that we have a 90% success rate in identifying potential leaders with this assessment tool. We have also been able to support existing and high potential leaders by applying our four-step learning and dilemma reconciliation process in action learning workshops and executive development sessions for many of our customers. A discussion some years ago with Michael Dell on the subject of dilemma reconciliation in anticipation of the publication of our book *21 Leaders for the 21st Century* (2001, McGraw-Hill) prompted Dell to say that he could use the dilemma methodology to leverage his own intuition to his management team. After several workshops and coaching sessions with us an HSBC executive began opening management team meetings by posing a dilemma that he needed the team to address. These leaders have the ability to facilitate the process of reconciliation, helping them to get the best out of their teams, particularly on issues requiring some form of integration or innovation.

What binds us? What divides us? What do we do to integrate?

In this book we take the reconciling strategy of "riding high," where the best of all worlds are synergistically combined. This process unfolds when there is at least as much attention on what organizations share as on what makes them different. This process is like a pendulum: it can swing at the bottom of diversity, because it is anchored at the top. The strength of that anchor indicates the agility of the values. The quality of the pendulum string signifies the quality of management and leadership. During a merger and acquisition, all three areas are under stress and need to be addressed thoroughly in order to create both innovative and organic growth from the integration process. Only if this happens during the very first 100 days of a merger will the merger be a success.

Our process is founded on the Trinity Approach[4] and it consists of three main perspectives:

Area 1: What binds and keeps us connected?
What we <u>stand for</u> and decide to <u>go for</u>: this enables us to generate a vision and values framework for the NEWCO organization.

Area 2: What separates and keeps us apart?
How we deal with the dilemmas resulting from diversity in vision and (cultural) values between the partner organizations involved.

Area 3: What should we do to benefit from the first and manage the second?
• "Live" the vision and values framework and create common behavior.
• Reconcile business dilemmas and create "win-win solutions."
• Develop key leadership behaviors: awareness, respect, courage, willpower, humility, discipline and "walking the talk."

The Trinity Approach ensures that the culture and corporate values of any NEWCO are integrated and redefined and that these support the (re)fined vision and mission of the organization. Reconciling the differences between the previous corporations builds a common platform for human capital, core values, talent management, leadership behavior, executive development, branding, and many business

---

4   We owe a great deal to Allard Everts, a senior consultant at THT.

processes for the future. The culture and business development process mobilizes energy, motivation and commitment from all staff in times of integration and change. In this way, a sustainable, future-oriented corporate identity is created supporting the strategic rationale and market position of the NEWCO.

Maximum performance from the integration is only achieved when strategic, structural, human resource, supplier and client processes are systemically aligned. In this wider context, our new approach is defined as a process of reconciling divergent goals, values, structural, functional and cultural differences for maximum performance.

CONCLUSION

Today's business world is complex and simplistic approaches to integration do not work, which is why too many mergers fail to realize the expected benefits. We have developed a portfolio of comprehensive solutions to help client organizations truly reach their hyperculture and thus realize and sustain the business benefits of their merger, acquisitions and alliances. All our consulting and leadership learning approaches are co-created with our clients using codified process steps that are tailored to our clients' specific needs. We aim to transfer the knowledge embedded in this process to our clients so that their ongoing and future operations continue to benefit under their own leadership and management.

We want to emphasize that this approach is not simply a matter of avoiding conflict, misunderstanding, and embarrassment, but a method of using differences to reach a higher level and deliver business benefits through connecting different viewpoints. The task of leaders is that of continuously co-creating with management and connecting viewpoints that are hard to connect. We hope we have helped you to identify the underlying value orientations of such viewpoints and the natural tensions between these that need to be recognized, respected, and subsequently reconciled to obtain and realize the required benefits from the integration. Being able to map these tensions on reproducible strategic grids that actually measure the gaps that need to be closed but are also very intuitive, helps to move organizations towards an understanding of joint goals and the creation of a common language—both crucial to achieving success in any type of business integration.

We have created a measurable set of tools that, when properly sequenced, can offer a sustainable human integration process that includes living the vision, mission, values paradigm while addressing the most salient integration challenges or dilemmas in a transparent yet directed manner. The process can be led by skilled managers who themselves can be assessed on their ability to create value from integration of human efforts throughout all layers of the organization. We have found that aside from engaging in a consistent process, the most important elements of integration success are:

1   A sense of urgency
2   Executive leadership and commitment

Without these two it is hard to accomplish anything in an organization, let alone something as complex as an integration.

One of the great advantages of our work is that all leaders grasp the dilemma approach as soon as they are engaged in the initial phases of the process. Leaders are beset by dilemmas and are often quite skilled at resolving them. However, their skill is leveraged and exploited in our approach and we apply a multiplier to this ability. Another strong part of our process is the inherent need to redefine some of the fundamental elements of the strategic process of an organization, such as rebuilding the vision, creating the BHAG, and re-establishing the values as well as expressing these in explicit and "measurable" behaviors. As all this happens in a consistent manner, the process can serve multiple purposes and is not exclusively beneficial to mergers and acquisitions. The dilemma reconciliation process is frequently practiced in strategic leadership development sessions in an action learning approach to point out the various tensions underlying organizational challenges.

We hope our approach will help you on your own "Tango to Integration."

INDEX

Acquisitions, 2. *See also* Mergers
  defined, 4
  loss of managers following, 6
  meta-dilemma of, 16–19
  prices of companies acquired in, 5
  success of, 2–3
Action-centered leadership model, 146
Adair, John, 146
Adaptation, 144
  reconciliation between creativity and, 47
Adaptors, versus innovators, 122–27
Alliances, categorical types of extreme behaviors in, 17
Analysis, 144–45
Arthur Anderson, 80, 155
Assessment metrics, 2–3
Awareness
  cross-cultural, 140–41
  developing systemic, 24
  of human choices, 141
  "State of the Planet," 140

BACA (Austrian bank), 27–28, 38
Balanced scorecards, 117
Bank of America, merger with Merrill Lynch, 5, 8
Banking, 27–28, 38, 81
"Bear" culture, 16
"Bear hug," 16
Beauty case, 45–49, 56, 82, 118–19
Behaviors, translating values into, 97, 99
"Being overtaken" axis, 16
"Best of Both" program, 70
BHAG (big, hairy, audacious goal), 29, 30–31, 114
  approaches to discovery and eliciting of, 32–33

defining, 30, 31
examples of, 30–31
need of, to be challenging, 31
validation of, 34–35
Big business, global business expansion as, 2
"Blended learning" approach, 150
BOC Ltd, 29, 37, 38
  merger with Linde AG, 67–69, 88–89
Booz Allen Hamilton study of 2001, 3n, 5
Bottom-up versus Top-down, 89
Brickmann, 141
Business case, creation of, 23, 25–111
  business case for integration, 23, 110–11
  business challenge assessment, 23, 35–50
  choosing values and behavior, 23, 76–109
  purpose and value assessment, 23, 51–76
  redefining vision and mission, 23, 25–35
Business case for integration, 23, 110–11
Business challenge assessment, 23, 35–50
Business dilemmas
  business challenges assessment through, 23
  manifestation of, in mergers, 38–39
  process of reconciliation of, 174–75
  recognizing, 175–76
  reconciled, 172–74
  reconciliation of, 41, 178–79
  respecting, 176–77
  ten golden, 11, 164–68
  trust and resolving, 169–72

Business orientations
  realization and rooting of, 36
  recognition of different, 36
  reconciliation of, 36, 37–38
  respect for differences in, 36

Campofrío Food Group, 37, 54–55, 92, 93, 95
"Can-do" mentality, 33
Capital sources of emerging markets, 3
Cartesian approach, 177
Cascading approach, 31, 33
Case studies, 150
"Causal" indicators, 24, 117, 118–22
Centralization, 35
  versus decentralization, 37, 156, 178
Change/flexibility, 66
Checkland, Peter, 53
Choosing values and behavior, 23, 76–109
Cisco Systems, 2, 5, 17, 19, 31
Client needs, serving, 108
Client-orientation, 82–83
Co-opetition, 134
Collins, 26, 30n, 32, 51
Commitment, 93–94
Communication
  as business process, 9
  with employees, 9
  during mergers, 9–10
Compass (catering), 5
Conceptualization, 133
Consciousness
  perspective, 140
  worldly, 140
Consulting services company, merger with global computer company, 40–41, 43–44
Continuous reevaluation, 24, 151–52
Control, 144
"Core ideology," alignment between "envisioned future" and, 26
Core values, 15
  exploring, through metaphors, 95–99
  fine-tuning, 99–100
  necessity of, 77–78
  organization of, 97
  selecting, 76
Corning, 3
Corporate cultures
  effect on effectiveness, 57
  values and behaviors of, 56–57
Corporate efficiency, 66
Covey, Stephen, 154
Creativity, reconciliation between adaptation and, 47

Cronbach Alpha reliability analysis, 63
Cross-border mergers and acquisitions, 57
Cross-cultural awareness, 140–41
Cross-cultural perspective, 158
Cross-selling, 12
Cross-validating questions, 63
Cultural differences
  as reason for merger failure, 8
  recognizing, 138–40
Cultural diversity, 57
Cultural due diligence, 178
Cultural inertia, recognizing, 116
Cultural integration, strategy of managing, 16–17
Cultural issues, resolving, 8–9
Culture
  building of trust and integration of the dimensions of, 162–68
  values and, 55–57
Culture Compass OnLine (CCOL), 150
Culture space, 177
Customer focus, 66
Customer satisfaction, 50
CVP (Corporate Values Profiler), 74

Decentralization, 35
  versus centralization, 37, 156n, 178
Decision-making
  differences in, 86–87
  quality and process of, 13–14
Deintegration process, 3
Dell, Michael, 182
Dialogue, integration of opposites as a continuous and creative, 49–50
Dilemma maps
  creation of, 9–10
  global, 179
Dilemma reconciliation processes (DRP), 99
Dilemmas. See Business dilemmas
DISA Group, merger of Wheelabrator and, 69–76
Discretion, 81
Discussion framework, 42
Distribution channel and supply chain analysis, 6
Diversity, 94–95, 173
  cultural, 57
Divestments, 3
DRP process, 50
Dual axis grid in assessing value orientation, 15, 162–63
Due diligence, 7
  cultural, 178
Dutch TNT Freight Management, 33

eBay, 31
EBITDA (earnings before interest, taxes, depreciation, and amortization), 5
Economies of scale, 12
Effectiveness, effect of corporate culture on, 57
Eiffel Tower culture, 61–64, 92
Emerging markets, capital sources of, 3
Employees
    communication with, 9
    retention of, 50
Enron, 80
Entrepreneurship, 94
"Envisioned future," alignment between "core ideology" and, 26
Everts, Allard, 183

Face-to-face interviews, 36
Fairness, 80
Family culture, 61, 63–64, 93, 126
Financial performance, 166
Financial services industry, deintegration in, 3
"Five times why" exercise, 53
Ford Motor, 30
Freedom, 81–82
Fukuyama, Francis, 154

General Electric, 2, 3, 31
Geodis Group, 33
    purchase of TNT Express, 39
Geodis Overseas, 33
Geodis Wilson, 33–35, 42–43, 115
Gerstner, Lou, 17
Giro Sport Design, 31
Global business expansion, as big business, 2
Global competitiveness, increase in, 3
Global computer company, merger with consulting services company, 40–41, 43–44
Global consciousness, 139
Global dilemmas, 179
Global dynamics, 141
    knowledge of, 141
Global sustainability, pressure of, 3
GM, 17
Goldensmith, Marshall, 116
Google, 31
Group, management of, 147
Group alignment and cohesion, 149
Group dialogue system, 35
Groupe Smithfield, 54, 55
Guided missile culture, 60, 63–64, 92, 126

Haier, 2, 3
Hamel, G., 30n
Hampden-Turner, C., 72, 143n, 158, 171n
Hands-on approach, 35
Hanvay, Robert G., 140, 141
Headcount reduction, 6
Helicopter view, 145
Hipple, Jack, 123
Honesty, 154
HSBC, 2
Human capital, 172
Human choices, awareness of, 141
Human dignity, respect for, 142
Human integration approach, mapping and measuring, 15–16
Human relationships
    basic assumptions and dimensions of, 158–60
    dimensions of, in building trust, 160–62
Human touch, 12
HVB (German bank), 27–28, 38

IBM, 2, 3, 5, 17, 31, 37
Identification of key drivers, 24, 113–16
Implementation strategy, developing, 24
    identification of key drivers in, 24, 113–16
    objectives and key performance indicators in, 24, 117–34
Incubator culture, 58–59, 63
Individuals
    creativity of, 144
    management of, 147
Initiation, 81
Initiatives, sustaining, 151
Innovator-Adaptor style inventory, 122
Innovators, adaptors versus, 122–27
Intact teams, 103–5
Integrated Kirton Questionnaire, 126
Integrated Type Indicators (ITIs), 124
Integrated value, 12
Integration, 4
    business case for, 11, 23, 110–11
    cultural challenge of, 4
    of process, 10
Integration leadership, 172–74, 179
Intercultural Assessment Profile (IAP), 72–73, 150
Intercultural competence, components of, 181
Intercultural competence graph, 139
Intercultural Competence Profiler (ICP), 137–48, 180
Internal Charter of Behavior, 102
Internet-chat, 56

Johnson & Johnson, 2, 3, 5
Joni, Saj-Nicole, 156n
Joyce, Robert E., Jr., 70
Justice, 80

Kelly, 142
Kenshiro Abbe 7th Dan, 52
Key driver identification, 24, 113–16
Key performance indicators (KPIs), 84
  developing implementation through,
    117–34
Key players, coaching of, 116
Key purpose statement, 114–15
Key reconciling indicators (KRIs), 117,
    121, 150
  on local-global orientation, 120
  on push and pull dilemma, 120
Kirton, M. J., 122–26
KPMG study of 1999, 5, 6, 9
Kuile, Pieter ter, 116

Laissez-faire approach, 35
Leaders
  dilemmas for, 14
  task of, 185
Leadership
  action-centered, 146
  integration, 172–74, 179
Learning, 66
  local, 107
Legacy companies
  culture of, 38
  decision-making approaches of,
    13–14
Lehman Brothers, 155
Lenovo, 2, 3
Likert scales, 125
Linde AG, 5, 26, 28–29, 37, 38, 90–91
  merger with BOC Ltd, 67–69, 88–89
Local-global orientation, key reconciling
  indicators (KRIs) on, 120
Local learning, 107
Loyalty/commitment, 66

Madoff, 155
Mahindra & Mahindra, 2, 3
Management competencies, 7
Management team, selection of, 7–8,
    9–10
Market reviews, 7
Market share, 50
Mass customization, 144
Mayo, Elton, 166n
Meetings, dilemmas about different
  ways of holding, 86–87

Mergers, 2
  categorical types of extreme behaviors
    in, 17
  challenges for organizations in, 5
  characteristics of successful, 10
  communication during, 9–10
  cultural differences as reason for
    failure of, 8
  defined, 4
  due diligence and, 7
  evaluating synergy and savings in, 6
  financial benefits of, 11
  goals of, 11
  key elements of success and failure, 5
  loss of managers following, 6
  manifestation of business dilemmas
    in, 38–39
  meta-dilemma of, 16–19
  price structure in, 5
  project planning integration, 7
  refining initial goals for, 25
  shareholder value and, 11
  success of, 2–3
  trust and communication during,
    158
Merrill, Rebecca, 154
Merrill Lynch, merger with Bank of
  America, 5, 8
Meta-dilemma of mergers and
  acquisitions, 16–19
Metaphors, exploring core values
  through, 95–99
Meyers-Briggs Type indicator (MBTI),
    124
Microsoft, 31
Mid Europa Partners, 69
Mission
  redefining, 23, 25–35
  values in giving life to, 90–91

New product development, 6
Non-operational pre-deal activities, due
  diligence and, 7
Norican Group, 69–76

Objectives, developing implementation
  through, 117–34
Old Mutual, 3
On-line semistructured questionnaires,
    36
Operational cost reductions, 6
Operational impact, 7
Opposites, integration of, as continuous
  and creative dialogue, 49–50
Organic growth strategy, 2

Organization Value Profiler (OVP), 34, 57–74, 92, 97
  change/flexibility, 66
  comparison of, with Personal Values Profiler (PVP), 115–16
  corporate efficiency, 66
  customer focus, 66
  Eiffel Tower, 61–64, 88, 92
  family, 61, 93, 126
  followers, 65
  guided missile, 60, 88, 92, 126
  incubator, 58–59
  learning, 66
  low performing, 64
  loyalty/commitment, 66
  market leaders, 65
  professional development, 66
  segments of, 59
  shareholder value, 66
  strategic alignment, 66
  structure, 66
  task orientation, 66
  teamwork, 66
Organizational identity renewal, 113
Organizational values as extensions of personal values, 91–95
"Outcome" indicators, 24, 117, 127–34
"Output" indicators, 24, 117, 122–27

Pan-European culture, problems of creating, 84
Passion, 144
People empowerment, 88
People integration, need for systematic and methodological framework of, 12–15
Performance indicators, 50
Personal alignment, 136–38
Personal trust, 157–58
Personal Value Profiler (PVP), 34, 74–76, 91–92, 97, 137, 148–49
  comparison of, with Organization Value Profiler (OVP), 115–16
Personal values, organizational values as extensions of, 91–95
Perspective consciousness, 140
Pfizer, 2
P&G, 2
PI/OL process, 56
Porras, 26, 30n, 32, 51
Power, attribution of, 173
Prahalad, C. K., 30n
Professional development, 66
Professional trust, 156–57

Profit making, elevating, 52
Profumo, Allessandro, 27, 77, 81–82
Project planning integration, 7
Purchase prices, as more realistic, 5
Purpose
  discovering the key, 52–53
  eliciting the key, 53, 55
  finding, 51–52
  value assessment and, 23, 51–76
  values in giving life to, 90–91
Push and pull dilemma, 145–46
  key reconciling indicators (KRIs) on, 120
PWC Consulting, 17, 37

Realization, 133, 138, 146
Realizing and rooting the benefits, 24, 135–52
  continuous reevaluation, 24, 151–52
  systemic alignment, 24, 135–49
  value and cultural awareness programs, 24, 150–51
Reciprocity, 81
Recognition, 138–40
Reconciled dilemmas, 172–74
Reconciliation, 19, 63, 133, 138, 143–46
  between creativity and adaptation, 47
Redefining vision and vision, 23, 25–35
Reitzle, Wolfgang, 26, 28, 67, 90
Relationship driven organizations, 40
Relationships, 94
Repeated questioning, 53
Research and development (R&D), 6, 83
Respect, 80, 138, 141–43
Responsibility, 81–82
Rew, Lynn, 141
"Riding high," reconciling strategy of, 182
Risk assessments, 7
Rohde & Liesenfeld, 33
ROI, 50
Root definition, 53

Savings, evaluating, 6
Self-awareness, 140
Self-determination, respect for rights to, 142–43
"Share for share" deals, 2
Shareholder value, 66, 83, 109, 166
  mergers and, 11
Shell, 145
Sheridan, Eileen, 140
Simulations, 150
SNCF (French railroad company), 33

Soft issues, 7
Sony, 30
The Speed of Trust: The One Thing That Changes Everything (Covey and Merrill), 154
Stakeholder value, 145
Standard, 144
"State of the Planet" awareness, 140
Strategic alignment, 66
Strategic alliances, 2. *See also* Mergers
    defined, 4
Structural alignment, 149
Structural trust, 156
Structure, 66
Style, 122–23
Supply chain consolidation, 12
Sustainability, 172–74
Synergy
    achieving, 49–50
    evaluating, 6
Synthesis, 144–45
Systemic alignment, 24, 135–49

"Take over" axis, 16
Talent management, 172
Task, achieving the, 146–47
Task orientation, 66
Tata & Sons, 2, 3
Team, management of, 147
Team spirit, 144
Teamwork, 66, 83, 106
Ten golden dilemmas, 11, 164–68
TNT Express, 42
Transnational organization, 144
Transparency, 81, 154
Triangulation, 8, 63
Trinity Approach, 183–84
Trompenaars, F., 72, 143n, 158, 171n
Trust, 80, 154–84
    building of, and integration of the dimensions of culture, 162–68
    dimensions of human relationships in building, 160–62
    motivators of, 159
    personal, 157–58
    professional, 156–57
    resolving dilemmas and, 169–72
    structural, 156
Trust: The Social Value and the Creation of Prosperity (Fukuyama), 154

Trust maps, 171
Trust pyramid, 157
Trustworthy relationships, 172
31 Leaders for the 21st Century, 182

"Unicorn" culture, 16
UniCredit, 26, 27–28, 38, 50, 77, 80, 81, 83
    future effectiveness of, 84
    Integrity Charter at, 78, 79
    meta-strategic dilemma of, 39
    vision of, 27

Value and cultural awareness programs, 24, 150–51
Value behavior choices, 23
Value orientations, 14–15
    dualities of, 15
Value-to-behavior (V2B) process, 100–103, 136, 149
Values
    acceptance of another culture's, 143
    as aid to reconciling key cultural dilemmas, 84–90
    conceiving, as integral verbs, 82–84
    culture and, 55–57
    in giving life to purpose and mission, 90–91
    organizational, as extensions of personal, 91–95
    translating into behaviors, 97, 99
Van der Zee, 141
Van Lennep, 145
Vision, redefining, 23, 25–35
Vodafone, 5

"Walk the talk," 136
Walmart, 30
"Water with the wine" position, 17
Wealth creation, 172
"WebCue," 36
Welch, Jack, 157–58
Wheelabrator, merger with DISA Group, 69–76
Who Says Elephants Can't Dance? (Gerstner), 17
Wilson Logistics, 33
Worldcom, 155
Worldly consciousness, 140

X-y grid, 16